60 is The New 40

The Ultimate Guide To Aging

Suzi Dent

ISBN: 978-0-6487295-6-3

DEDICATION

I dedicate this book to the love of my life, my son Jack.
You are an amazing young man and I'm so very proud of you.

Thank you to the following women who tribe with me,
I am ever so grateful that you are all in my life.

Tracey, Vicki, Alanna, Rita, Jacqueline, Barbie, Annette, Marie C, Marie B, Nicole, RoseAnne, Mandy, Penny, Julie OAM, Joanne, Jo, Melisa, Ellie, Layla, Kate, Melissa, Renee, Jacqui and Miss Sonia.

CONTENTS

INTRODUCTION

As the author of "60 is the New 40," I bring a unique blend of experience and expertise to the table. With years of work as a film and TV hair and makeup artist, I have a deep understanding of how to care for skin and hair.

Additionally, my background in manufacturing my own natural cosmetics has given me a wealth of knowledge about healthy products and ingredients.

As a wellbeing and empowerment coach, I am passionate about helping people achieve their best selves - physically, mentally, emotionally and spiritually. And as a dance fitness instructor, I know how important it is to keep your body moving and strong.

But perhaps most importantly, I live and breathe my message. At 60 years young, I look and feel better than ever before. And I am committed to sharing my knowledge and expertise with others, so that they too can feel empowered, vibrant, and full of life at any age.

In the pages ahead, I want to share my journey with you - the ups and the downs, the victories and the struggles - so that you can learn from my experiences and disrupt your own aging process.

Whether you want to make physical changes to your body, transform your mindset, or dive deeper into your spirituality, I am here to guide and support you every step of the way.

So let's embark on this journey together - one that is full of growth, healing, and empowerment.

Isn't Aging Interesting?

When we were little children in the sixties and seventies, our mothers told us "Don't be in a hurry to grow up! It will happen before you know it!" And they were right, it did. When we were little girls, our mothers didn't discuss boys and sex and periods and how babies were made and many of us were given a book, What every teenage girl should know, and there was one for boys too.

They were not as open about sexuality and we were raised to believe in modesty and chastity and to be a virgin when we were married. To save ourselves for "the one". The man that we had to marry that would look after us and take care of us, for we were raised to believe that we could not make it in this world without a man to take care of us.

Our duties were to produce babies and clean the house and do the cooking and look after our husband and the children. Not to have a career or any aspirations for one. Just a job.

When I was in my mid-twenties, with an excellent income, I wasn't allowed to have a housing loan by myself, I had to have a man go guarantor for me, he didn't even have to be a relative, any man would do because it was expected that I would soon be settling down and having babies.

I was also told that this would be happening by the male bank manager. The job and career I was working for didn't really count for anything, as if I was just biding my time until motherhood came. When we were little girls we were also told that children should be seen and not heard.

However, when I grew up, I realised that this was true for women too. Women were allowed to be seen, they were taught to dress a certain way, sit a certain way, and act a certain way. We were taught to not answer back, especially to men as that was rude and bossy and women should not be seen as this. We were taught that it wasn't safe to walk alone at night and that we had to tuck our keys in between our fingers.

We were taught that what we wore was important to our safety and how we were perceived in society, that if we showed our bra straps we could be seen as a loose woman with no morals and that was bad.

Women were seen and not heard when we walked past building sites full of men, who would stop work to yell obscene sexual things at us and whistle and catcall at us. They did this to us in our early teens and I used to avoid walking past them if I could because it was scary at 14. If I had to I would just put my head down and get past.

Yes, it was flattering when we were older as we had been programmed by then that we were supposed to enjoy it and that this was how men appreciated us and showed us that we were attractive.

We learnt that cars driving past us with men leering at us and calling out and whistling was supposed to bet met with an appreciative smile.

Women were seen and not heard when we went to the auto mechanic to get our cars serviced and we were greeted by leering male mechanics and a wall full of spread-legged pornography. Full on nudes that were in the office and on display for everyone to see.

I hated going to the mechanic when I was younger and because of this and how uncomfortable I felt, I would always get a male friend to take my car for me. Until one day I found a mechanic who had been taught by his 5 sisters to not do this and that women hated it and finally, I found a mechanic I felt safe taking my car to for its regular service. He was also a great mechanic.

We were seen and not heard when men touched us and felt us up without our permission because it was a man's right and boys will be boys, so we were taught to tolerate it with politeness, so as not to offend the men. We were raised to not say anything.

To smile politely and bear it whilst being a lady, because if we called them on their behaviour, that was apparently all our fault because of what we looked like and we were then called a bitch!

Women were not heard! Women were raised to be complacent and quiet and to go along with what society dictated to us.

This mainly came from the media, which back then, surprise surprise, was all run by men. But over the decades women have started to wake up, to use their voices to speak up loudly in protest, to disrupt the status quo! To be heard and not just seen. We saw actresses who stood up, women who we could admire and idolise as our role models.

We experienced the rise of feminism and equal rights and opportunities for women and over the decades, we experienced more and more employment opportunities being offered to women.
We applauded and were proud of the changing face of the western world for women, different from our mothers and grandmothers days, when they were not even considered being worthy to vote, because of their gender.

One thing that did not change however, was the society of disbelief that we lived in. Where sexual assaults were still rife and men would continue to touch us without our consent, as if it was their god given right.

Where women were blamed for what they were wearing, how they acted, whether they were drinking etc etc and men were still not questioned in the same way for why they had behaved the way they did. Women didn't often come forward in sexual assault cases and rape cases, because they would be the ones that were blamed and so they often suffered in silence.

In 2014 there was a huge police operation headed up by Scotland Yard in the UK, that changed the world for women.

It targeted the entertainment industry, a place where men ruled and money and power, and position was the currency of choice. This industry had no rules of behaviour, not like the corporate world, and was full of the glitz and glamour of superstars.

We loved the entertainers who filled our television screens, who we welcomed into our homes to delight us and our children with their songs, their comedy, their on-screen personas, and men who were idolised.

Operation Yewtree was the first of its kind that actually delved deep into decades of complaints of sexual assaults by male superstars that had been ignored or swept under the rug. This was the first time in our history that survivors of historical crimes were not just seen, but they were listened to, heard and believed.

In 2014 I decided that I wanted to be heard and I came forward as a bad character witness in the Rolf Harris pedophile court case. I came forward in support of the women who were little girls when he sexually molested them. I came forward because when I was 23 he assaulted me at work, surrounded by other men, my workmates who supported him and his actions by their absence of voice. Who were intimidated by his stardom, his power, and his position in this world. When I was 23 in 1986 and his makeup artist, I wasn't allowed to use my voice either.

I had to be polite and smile whilst this dirty old man pawed at me and groped me and touched my body for his own pleasure. From that day forward, he was the last man that I ever allowed to touch me without my permission. I continued my habit of dressing down like a tomboy, wearing baggy clothes and never anything figure-hugging, no dresses or anything sleeveless, because I felt that I moved through life safer that way and that's how I dressed and who I became for the next 30 years of my life.

In 2014 I was chosen by the judge as a bad character witness in his trial, one of six including one man, for I had never kept my assault a secret. I took the stand and I was heard. I was called the strongest bad character witness for the prosecution by the press around the world. My voice mattered, It mattered for me, for the other women who had testified with me, and as it turned out, for women around the world.

That day in court changed my life. We were all granted lifetime anonymity by the British court for our own safety, because back then, society was shocked to its very core! People were not ready to believe that Rolf Harris was a pedophile and millions of people around the world got their Suzi hate on.

Keyboard warriors with an opinion, as if seeing him on television and growing up watching him on their screens meant that they knew him. People weren't ready to accept that he was a sexual abuser of girls and young women so they did what society has always done for generations, they blamed the women. We were all lying, doing it for the money, the fame!

There was no way that England's national treasure and Australia's favourite son Rolf Harris was anything but an upstanding citizen, he was a friend of the royal family!
He had painted the queen for goodness sake! It was a huge moment for me, stepping up and speaking out in support of myself and others, because when I was 12, I was sexually assaulted for the first time and inside that courtroom,

my 12 year old girl who had stayed silent for so long, was egging me on and she was there with other little girls, a nine year old, an eleven year old and a fifteen year old, all grown into adult women and none of our little girls would let us be silent anymore!

It is our responsibility as older women in society to raise our daughters to have a voice and our sons to be the men we want them to be and respect women. Children are a product of their upbringing and the outdated generational mode of behaviour that we have been raised with is also our responsibility to stamp out.

Women can now be anything they want to be and the glass ceiling that once chopped women's heads off really no longer exists. As we have aged we have seen and experienced women's liberation in many countries of the world and in 2017 we all saw and experienced the biggest global healing movement for women that the world has ever seen!

That hashtag #metoo was shared on millions of social media profiles really fast around the world. What it represented to us all was huge! For some women, this was the very first time they had ever admitted that they had been assaulted, but the solidarity of standing with millions of sisters around the world was a catalyst for action, and the healing journeys for many women and some men started on that day.

My personal healing journey and my catalyst for change, happened one week after that history-making court case, that found rolf harris guilty and sent him to prison for his crimes.

Throughout my journey, I have had the privilege of being able to connect with and listen to many brave and courageous individuals who have reached out to me after seeing my interviews on TV and in print.
It has been an honour and a blessing to be trusted with their stories of sexual abuse and assault.

Some of these individuals have shared their story for the very first time, and for that, I am incredibly grateful.

As I reflect on my experiences, I realise that I have grown and learned so much. That is why I am thrilled to share with you my journey of how to disrupt your aging process physically, mentally, emotionally, and spiritually. I hope that my journey can inspire and empower you to make positive changes in your own life.

Menopause and Marriage

At 51 my hips ached, my body was sweaty, my sleep was not good and my moods erratic. I got a starburst fracture in my knee cap just from squatting down in an odd way. My husband told me, when I went to have a blood test, that there had better be something wrong with me or he was divorcing me.

He was angry all the time frustrated at his own life and in the habit of taking it all out on me. I felt like I was on a train, that never stopped to let me off and it was a life filled with debt and frustration and no hope of any change at all. It was a Groundhog Day of sameness every day and I was very unhappy.

I felt that it was my duty as his wife to let him vent at me, to spew all his anger and hatred and disappointment in life at me and into me. And he would do it all the time.

He would be up all night working himself up into a rage and then when I woke up, he would talk at me, over and over round and round until he was empty and then he would go and sleep.

This happened in cycles and it was every week then several times a week then it happened all the time. Nothing I did was good enough. I could never help him with his business enough, he worked from home and never left.
   He would accuse me of being the death of him, that everything in our lives was somehow my fault. I didn't clean enough I didn't help him enough. I was not enough.

He gas lit me and was controlling and confrontational. His communication style was as an interrupter and he would never let me finish a sentence. He was constantly moody and would sleep a lot of the day not waking until lunchtime and then he would either be in a good mood when he woke up, or he would have carried something forward from a previous day to be pissed off about.

I didn't answer back or push his buttons to make any of this happen, because that would just trigger more anger from him, he was just an angry person. He never used to be.

Often, when he hadn't woken by 2pm I would think that he had died from the amount of substances he was taking and I would listen at the door to see if I could hear him breathing. I would never open the door.

As his wife and a woman who was losing herself, I actually loved him, more than I loved myself. I just didn't realise it at the time. In hindsight I know now that many of us feel this way because of our upbringing and how we have been raised.

To always put family before oneself is a kind of innate thing in many women, at the expense of our own mental and emotional health. We are last on our list of self care and put everyone in the family first. Its a societal expectation.

We had been together for 21 years by this time and I was used to his emotional outbursts, but you can only tolerate this sort of behaviour for so long before it starts to weigh you down and hurt your soul. I always used to tell him positive things and try to uplift him and it worked a lot of the time for many years.

I would tell him that he just hadn't reached his full potential yet whilst he kept offloading on me and a lot of it became just made up lies from him because he became paranoid and enjoyed yelling.
He was messy and erratic and had a toxic energy about him that filled the house. It was an uncomfortable environment to live in.

We didn't sleep in the same bedroom which was great, so at least I had my own space to sleep in and watch tv and my own bathroom. My oasis, full of my loving vibe and my joyous energy, so our son used to come and hang in my room with me and we felt safe and calm up there.

I also worked as a freelance film and tv hair and makeup artist, something I had done since I was 21. So I earned money and contributed to our lives, and I would come home and go to my room. I ate there, slept there, dreamt and manifested there and worked there. But still, I was never enough.

Many of us turn to different vices to fill the emotional void when we are not receiving the right energy in our lives from our significant others. We drink alcohol, comfort eat all the things we know we are not supposed to. We smoke cigarettes or we turn to drugs. We can also get prescribed anti depressants to put a bandaid over our feelings so we cruise through life in another numb way.

My vices were not alcohol, but an on again off again love affair with food. Which around this time saw me drop to my lowest weight ever at 63.5 kilos. I was very skinny for me, lost all my curves, had no bum, which was uncomfortable to sit on as I was boney and my breasts shrunk and sagged.

Naked I looked sick and I controlled my weight by eating 2 protein bars a day, that was it and I was on the scale everyday, enjoying on the inside that I was skinny and that this was the only thing I seemed to have control of in my life.

The other thing I did was smoking, both cigarettes and marijuana. My husband always saw to it that I had a plentiful supply as he is an enabler, so even when I wanted and needed to cut down or stop my habit, he would not let that happen. He liked me better stoned all the time and I was more zen that way and more able to cope with him and his moods.

He had developed an anger management problem and an attitude of blame and to be quite honest, being stoned was the only way I was coping with my life. I have to add here that I am a highly functional stoned person and know one ever knew that I was using, unless I told them. The cigarettes I only ever did at home, never took them with me as it was a way of coping in my living environment. It was also out of control.

My blood test showed that my hormone levels had dropped so low that the progesterone was leaching from my bones, the only way I could describe it at the time, thus the fracture. I spent the next 16 months on crutches with knee problems and hip pain and for 2 weeks I was completely bed ridden as I was only comfortable when I lay down. My body was letting me down and I couldn't walk up stairs and used to bum it up the stairs to get to my bedroom to lie down. It was not good and very debilitating.

I had gone from being very fit at 46 and becoming a jazzercise dance fitness instructor to having a body that was letting me down. In only a few years. All due to menopause and the changes in hormone levels. I had to give up the dancing, because my knees wouldn't let me. Im sure the emotional trauma I was subjected to and living in a constant state of walking on eggshells around my husband, was not helping either.

Friends didn't drop in anymore, I only left the house to go to work as I was needed at home and casual clients would come to my studio to have their hair and makeup done. We lived a very secluded life and rarely went out as he couldn't be in public and wouldn't leave the house. When he did, either my son or I would have to go with him. Life was difficult to say the least and this had been going on for several years by now.

Going through menopause and peri menopause is like being in puberty on steroids.

It sneaks up on you in your mid to late 40's and you often have no idea at all that your body has started its journey of change. When my fracture occurred and I had my first blood test with the ultimatum of divorce attached to it, my husband changed his attitude towards me immediately when finding out the results of my vanishing hormone levels.

He took it upon himself to research all he could about hormones and amino acids and different healthier ways to help me cope with menopause. We have both always been into health and fitness and I was a project for him. And he found out lots of information and had me on a regimen of natural therapies and amino acids designed to build my bones, calm my anxiety, help with my sleep and improve my health.

He was very supportive and discovered many nutrients that would benefit my journey. We had a lot of love for each other and when he was calm and loving our relationship was great.

My menopause journey set me on a path of rebuilding my health and fitness and living a pain free life. I share all the remedies that I discovered that have worked really well for me and others that I have always used over the years, that have supported my skin and hair health on my life journey.

Midlife Moods

 One evening my husband and I were watching a current affairs type programme and saw an interview with a woman who was taking Rolf Harris to court for sexually molesting her when he was 15. I watched with great fascination as I knew without a shadow of doubt that she was not lying. However society and the press at the time were poking holes in her story and judging her for having a publicist who had received payment for her story.

That night I did some googling and reached out to the uk to come forward in support of her as I hate injustice and I hate that women are not believed when they have been sexually assaulted. I never kept my day being groped by a dirty old man a secret and now when it counted the most, I sure was not going to keep quiet.

I never asked permission or told my husband until I had heard from the police in charge of the case and I had started the ball rolling. He never tried to stop me in my quest to see justice happen as he knows who I am and how passionate I am when I decide to advocate for something or someone.

I have done many interviews about my part in the case and I'm proud to be one of the 9 brave, strong confident women that stepped up, spoke out and helped jail him and I hope that the others got some sort of healing and closure for coming forward. We were all given lifetime anonymity from the British courts for our protection, as millions of people were in complete shock and because of the culture of disbelief towards women, they believed we were all lying and were doing it for the money. Fyi there was no money on offer, we did it to see justice done.

I've never disclosed to anyone in any of my interviews what I was going through at the time and what my life was like, because it wasn't pertinent to the story and no-one ever asked. My father had died only 6 months previously and I had gone non contact with my narcissistic toxic, manipulative, controlling mother and removed her from my life as well.

My hips gave me a lot of pain when I sat for too long and the flight from Australia is a very long way. I was in a lot of pain when I was there and was rubbing anti inflammatory cream on my hips and glutes several times a day, to ease the pain of walking. I was staying in a hotel that had a pool and a spa and every morning and evening I would sit in the spa with the water jets massaging my hips to ease the pain, which helped a lot.

The very next morning, after my turn on the witness box in court. I had returned to my room after my pool spa and had just had a shower to get ready for the day and my husband called.

He was livid and had worked himself into a real state of anger, he verbally abused and attacked me on the phone and I fainted and just lay on the floor sweating in my towel whilst his abuse and his anger just washed over me and through me. It was awful and I have learnt that this is a direct trauma response to being attacked.

We have the fight , flight, freeze, fawn or flop as a response to trauma. My body and my whole emotional system was so overwhelmed with him verbally abusing me for years and the enormity of being part of the biggest court case of this kind in the world.

Add to that all the emotions of the past six months, that my system overloaded and I collapsed to the floor, overwhelmed with the stress. It was a complete turning point in my relationship with him and several times more in the month that I was away, he verbally abused and attacked me over the phone.

When I was there in England, it was the first time in a very long time that I finally felt free. It was an amazing feeling to feel a sense of freedom, you can kind of taste it and it was wonderful to experience and I let it fill my body, as I enjoyed not having him near me and I just loved that I was there, with a friend to support me.

My life started to change when I was there and I learnt a lot about my menopausal, emotional, physical and spiritual self at 52 and I began my healing journey.

It was inside the ancient spiritual stone walls of Stone Henge, in England. one week after the now historic court case against Rolf Harris, that this happened. It was dawn and very cold, a beautiful English morning with no rain.

Stonehenge stood before me in all its majesty, these huge monolithic rocks in a rough-hewn circle. Michael, my special guide and shamanic healer, led me through the ancient entrance to the stones following the pathway my ancestors would have walked. I felt so heavy inside, with what was going on in my life and the enormity of the case and my words being printed all around the world.

However, I felt such peace and spirituality emanating from the stones. It was an amazing feeling and I knew that I was exactly where I should be, I felt like it had been ordained. I walked around the stones just breathing deeply and being present in the moment, feeling a sense of belonging that I can't explain.

Michael performed a sacred, spiritual ceremony, whilst we sat on the ground inside the circle and I felt more present mentally, spiritually, and emotionally than I ever had in my entire life and he blessed me with water from the chalice well.

The tears flowed out of me, bucket loads uncontrollably, as all the anguish and anger, years of pent-up emotions, and the burden and shame I had carried within me since I was 12, came gushing out of me. I forgave all those that had wronged me in my life, all the times I had been sexually abused and all those feelings of low self worth that I had attached to those moments in time.

Forgiveness is so important in our healing journey. When we forgive those who have abused us, we do it not for them, but to free ourselves.

With the tears came this huge emotional release, like a tap had been turned on. The sun rose streaming through the gaps in the stones and bathed us with its warm light.

It was obvious to those close to me that I had undergone a huge healing and had been changed. I was filled with happiness light, a bright golden light. I felt amazing, so alive, like I had been blessed. My soul and my heart and my head were no longer heavy but had a lightness and emptiness.

The anger that I had carried around with me for decades was being replaced by joy. I was no longer angry, I was being filled with such a feeling of peace and happiness, even my facial features changed that day and I was a younger, lighter-looking me.

Just as a caterpillar must go through a transformative process in order to become a butterfly, women and men can also experience a period of transformation during their midlife transition. Often there is a trigger point like I experienced in Stonehenge.

The emotional baggage that you have been storing in the dusty suitcase in your mind, that you haven't dealt with yet, can suddenly be triggered and come flooding back and if you have not dealt with it before now, you will be forced to now.

This is where having a trusted coach and advisor can be so very important to your life journey. We can't do this life alone, we need the right people around us, who see us, hear us, have been us and can relate to our issues and struggles.

Menopause is a natural and normal part of a woman's life, but it can also be a challenging time. Many women experience a variety of symptoms, including hot flashes, mood swings, and sleep disturbances. While these symptoms can be difficult to deal with, it's important to communicate them to your family.

It can help them understand what you're going through.
This includes your spouse, children, and other loved ones who may be living with you or close to you. By sharing your experiences, you can help them understand what you are going through and how they can support you.

Menopause can cause mood swings and irritability, which can be confusing for your family members. By explaining the reason behind your behaviour, you can help them be more patient and understanding.

It also encourages open communication. Menopause is still a taboo topic in many cultures, and women may feel embarrassed or ashamed to talk about it. By starting the conversation with your family, you can break down these barriers and encourage more open communication.

By sharing your symptoms with your family, you can feel validated and supported, knowing that you are not alone.

The midlife transition can be a challenging and sometimes uncomfortable process, as we navigate the physical, emotional, and social changes that come with aging.

Like a chrysalis, women during this time undergo a process of change and growth, as they shed their old selves and emerge transformed.

However, just as the butterfly emerges from its chrysalis more beautiful and vibrant than before, women can also emerge from this transformative period with newfound strength, wisdom, and beauty.

During this time, women will often reflect on their lives, reassess their goals and priorities, and make changes that allow them to live more fully and authentically. You may discover new passions, form deeper connections with loved ones, and embrace your unique strengths and gifts.

While the midlife transition can be a time of uncertainty and change, it can also be a time of great growth and transformation. Like the butterfly emerging from its chrysalis, you have the potential to spread your wings and soar, embracing all the possibilities and opportunities that life has to offer.

MID LIFE CHANGES IN MEN

This communication also goes both ways. Your aging male partner can also be experiencing mid life issues with his health, his hormones and his feelings. Midlife hormonal changes in men are a natural part of the aging process, typically occurring between the ages of 40 and 60.

These changes are largely due to declining levels of the male hormone testosterone, which can lead to a variety of physical and psychological symptoms. Some of the common changes are:

Decrease in testosterone levels: Men experience a gradual decline in testosterone levels with aging, which can lead to a decrease in sexual desire, energy levels, and muscle mass.

Erectile dysfunction: Midlife hormonal changes in men can also lead to erectile dysfunction (ED), which is the inability to achieve or maintain an erection.

Loss of muscle mass and strength: Testosterone plays a critical role in maintaining muscle mass and strength, so as testosterone levels decrease, men may experience a loss of muscle mass and strength.

Increased body fat: Lower testosterone levels can also lead to an increase in body fat, particularly around the waistline.

Mood changes: Men may experience mood changes such as irritability, depression, and fatigue.

Decreased bone density: Testosterone is also important for maintaining bone density, so low levels of testosterone can lead to decreased bone density and an increased risk of fractures.

If your partner is experiencing any of these symptoms, it is important to talk to your doctor to determine if they are related to midlife hormonal changes or if there may be another underlying cause. Your doctor may recommend hormone replacement therapy or other treatments to help alleviate his symptoms.

Age is Just a Number

Age really is just a number and it's at this mid life stage that we really must embrace this as our mantra. Many of us start to give up a bit when we are in our mid 50's. We can get a bit slack about our diets and exercise regime and can start to fall into a complacency pattern.

Especially if we are in a long term relationship and feel very comfortable. We see it all the time and society calls this "letting ourselves go". This happens in both men and women. Physically we see it as the middle aged spread that starts to occur in all of us around this age.

When we are younger our metabolism's are so much faster and we burn fat quicker are more agile and our bones are not cracking and creaking in places. It's around this time of life that many changes in our body dynamics are really starting to be felt and we often feel that this is all a normal part of aging and just accept it.

Mentally many of us strive for new things. We change jobs, change direction in life, challenge ourselves by getting university degrees and further education. We learn new skills and often turn to self employment as a better option.

Sometimes though, we may be feeling unfulfilled or not heard in our relationships with our partners and our children and sometimes with our long term friends.

Feeling walked over emotionally means feeling like your emotions and needs are disregarded or invalidated by others. It's the feeling that someone is taking advantage of your kindness, empathy, or willingness to help without reciprocating or respecting your feelings.

When you feel walked over emotionally, it can lead to feelings of resentment, anger, and sadness. You may feel like you're always the one making sacrifices, compromising, or putting others' needs before your own. Over time, this can lead to emotional exhaustion and burnout.

If you're feeling walked over emotionally, it's important to set boundaries and communicate your needs clearly. It's okay to say no to things that don't align with your values or priorities. Practice self-care and prioritise your own well-being to avoid burnout.

2016 found me in a toxic co-dependent marriage, very unhappy, feeling desperate, not enough, unfulfilled and without hope or purpose. Stuck in the proverbial dark tunnel without hope and with no light to turn toward for salvation, I was out of balance and my naturally bright light was really dim.

I needed to fill up my spiritual gas tank and so I started to listen to motivational speakers on my daily walks and the one thing I learnt was that to really change your life, you had to make yourself uncomfortable.

I decided to pray, have faith, trust my instincts and reach out to God / the universe with both hands to show me what I needed to learn and experience to change my life. Be careful what you wish for though, because the universe often has much bigger plans in store for you.

I remember listening to Oprah once talk about listening to the whispers of the universe. It's when thoughts pop into your head and you think oh, that sounds odd, that doesn't make any sense. However if you don't pay attention to the whispers of the universe, they get louder and louder until you do.

I started to pay attention and listened to the whispers and was sent a message right out of left field when I was approached to be a contestant in an international beauty pageant, Mrs Earth Australia.

I nearly fell off the bed laughing! I told them I was 55 and they said that older women did take part. I had been a tomboy for 30 years, never wearing dresses and heels or fitted anything. I had a psychological fear of frocks and felt very uncomfortable wearing them.

But I payed attention to this very odd message and checked them out. They supported a charity that I was impressed by who collected new and used shoes to distribute around the world to those who didn't have any.

I realised that my husband could participate as he was in the international transport industry and whilst I thought about it I received a whole download of how I could do this and the business I could contact to help me support this charity.

I also realised I was in my very own sliding doors moment. I could stay where I was, in a miserable existence or I could say yes and bring something different into my life and my marriage.

So I said yes and in doing so I changed my life.

I raised awareness for the charity and supported them on their fundraising journey, I spoke on their behalf at functions and on podcasts and on television.

I pushed through my fears, one dress at a time, and had full faith and confidence that I was on the right life path. My husband was very supportive and enjoyed buying me dresses online and loved the new me.

I practised daily gratitude had 100% self-belief and everyday I used manifestation techniques and visualised being on stage and hearing my name called out as the winner. Every day I would play the scenario in my head where I heard my name called whilst standing back stage… Mrs Earth Australia the winner is Suzi Dent! I would fill myself up with the joy and gratitude that I would feel as if it had already happened.

I had business sponsorship and dress and cosmetic sponsors and a fitness trainer who got me in great shape and I shed the weight I had put back on and felt fit and strong in my body again.

I practised wearing high heels every day by standing at the end of my bed on the carpet, to get my balance for a week before I actually walked in them. Then the next three weeks were just on carpet as I was worried about loosing my balance on the six inch heels, before I graduated myself to tiles and wooden flooring.

I succeeded in my goals and went on to be crowned the first Mrs Earth Australia 2017, which was amazing! My husband and I had new found zest to our marriage and by overcoming my fears and body issue problems, I had built my self-esteem to the high levels of my confidence. In doing so I had discovered my true authentic self.

I found myself in Vegas a few months later, representing Australia, where I competed against 36 other women from around the globe, half of whom I could have given birth to and I was crowned 3rd as Mrs Earth Health.

I received press all around the world as the 55-year-old tomboy to beauty queen and was on national morning tv and radio shows, the news, international and local magazines and in newspapers and on podcasts.

I'm delighted to say that my personal transformation journey has inspired many other women to enter the world of pageantry and follow their dreams.

The doors of motivational speaking opened to me and I found myself in 2019 speaking at the Womens Economic Forum in India with 2000 other women, where I won an international speaking award as a woman of substance. All because I said YES to the whispers and stepped into action.

Today, the reason I am an empowerment and well-being coach, working with women who are just like who I used to be, is because I've learnt that this world needs strong women who can transform it.

So please, don't discard yourself and believe that you are too old to do something, just because society dictates that it is so. There is no handbook that teaches any of us how to behave, how to dress and who to be.

We are our own authentic selves and by being so we can truly empower ourselves to reach our full potential. Living our lives and setting a positive and empowering example for others our own age and younger to follow.

Communication

I feel that many adults of both sexes could benefit from an upgrade in their communication skills. To be more introspective of their past relationships and look at them more as a learning and growing experience.

Adopting the mantra of "well this is me, take it or leave it, I'm too old to change" is counterproductive and counterintuitive.
No one is ever too old to learn and grow. We all have baggage, but we don't need to take it all with us to another relationship.

We can pop it in storage for a while and look at it every now and again, as we may need reminders of where we have come from.
I believe life is about learning and growing and working on oneself to be better, to do better. To be more. To do more.

Life is short. Bring the evolved you into any new relationship, not the old one. Learning and growing is what life is all about.

Good communication skills are essential in today's world. Whether you're interacting with colleagues at work, talking with friends and family, or giving a presentation, being a good communicator can help you build stronger relationships, convey your ideas more effectively, and achieve your goals. I have seen grown women share way too much on social media and completely destroy their relationships. Don't air your dirty laundry in public, as my grandmother used to say.

Good communication starts with active listening. Pay attention to what the other person is saying, and don't interrupt or assume you know what they're going to say. Instead, ask questions and clarify your understanding to make sure you're on the same page.

Being a good listener is an essential skill for building strong and healthy relationships, both personal and professional. It involves actively paying attention to the person speaking, understanding their perspective, and responding in a thoughtful and empathetic manner.

When we listen attentively to others, we demonstrate respect, empathy, and understanding. We show that we value their thoughts, feelings, and opinions, and that we are willing to take the time to truly understand them. This can help to build trust and rapport, and create a more positive and harmonious relationship.

Being a good listener can also help to improve our communication skills. When we listen carefully to others, we can pick up on subtle cues and signals that can help us better understand their needs and expectations.
We can then respond in a way that is more appropriate and effective, which can help to prevent misunderstandings, conflicts, and hurt feelings.

Moreover, being a good listener can help us to learn and grow as individuals. By listening to the experiences and perspectives of others, we can broaden our own knowledge and understanding, and gain new insights and perspectives. This can help us to become more open-minded, empathetic, and compassionate, which can have a positive impact on all aspects of our lives.

When you're speaking, be clear and concise in your message. Avoid using jargon or technical terms that the other person may not understand, and try to use simple language. Organise your thoughts beforehand, so that you can express yourself clearly and concisely.
Non-verbal communication is just as important as verbal communication. Use body language to convey your message, such as maintaining eye contact, using gestures, and having an open posture. This will help you convey confidence and sincerity.

Put yourself in the other person's shoes and try to understand their perspective. Be empathetic, this will help you communicate more effectively and build stronger relationships. Encourage the other person to share their thoughts and feelings by asking open-ended questions. Give active feedback to demonstrate that you're listening, and summarise the other person's points to show that you understand their perspective.

Be open to new ideas and perspectives, and be willing to change your mind if the evidence supports it. Avoid getting defensive or closed-minded, as this can hinder communication and damage relationships. Even in difficult or emotionally charged situations, try to stay calm and respectful. Avoid attacking the other person, and focus on the issues rather than the person.

Miscommunication occurs when there is a failure to understand or convey a message effectively. It can happen in any communication setting, whether it's in personal relationships, work environments, or any other social interaction. Miscommunication can lead to misunderstandings, confusion, and even conflict.

If the individuals involved in a conversation speak different languages, there can be misunderstandings due to cultural differences, idiomatic expressions, or nuances in language. Sometimes, people may use words or phrases that have multiple meanings, or they may interpret things differently due to personal biases or preconceptions.

Nonverbal cues such as facial expressions, body language, and tone of voice can significantly impact the meaning of a message. Make sure you are paying attention visually as well as listening.

Interrupting someone while they are speaking can be disrespectful and can undermine the speaker's confidence and ability to express themselves. It can also prevent the listener from fully understanding the speaker's message, which can lead to misunderstandings and conflicts.
When we interrupt others, we send a message that we are more interested in our own thoughts and opinions than in what the other person has to say.

This can create a power dynamic that can make the other person feel unheard and undervalued, which can harm the relationship.
Moreover, interrupting can prevent us from fully understanding the other person's perspective, which can limit our own knowledge and understanding. When we interrupt, we cut off the flow of communication and miss out on important information and insights.

Being an interrupter means frequently cutting off or talking over someone who is speaking. Interrupting someone can be a common behaviour, but it can also be a sign of poor communication skills and lack of respect for the person speaking.

Interrupting someone can be frustrating for both the speaker and the listener.

When someone interrupts, it can break the flow of the conversation and make it difficult to fully understand what the speaker is trying to convey. It can also create tension and lead to misunderstandings or arguments.
Interrupting can also send a message to the speaker that their thoughts and opinions are not valued or important. This can be harmful to a relationship, as it can make the speaker feel disrespected or unheard.

My husband would interrupt me constantly, would never let me finish a sentence. I would completely loose my train of thought or what I was even trying to say. It made me feel undervalued and bullied in the relationship. I eventually got so tired of his behaviour that I barely spoke to him and certainly not about anything that was meaningful to me.

I was driven to the point of having to raise my voice and my hand in the stop signal and tell him to shut up, that I had not finished speaking and to stop interrupting. This was not a proactive way to communicate, but came from him causing a confrontational moment from his desire to control and dominate.

It is disempowering to be with an interrupter, their arrogance in communicating like this and their own sense of self importance dominates the conversation, so much so that it can really affect any relationship, personal or business in a detrimental way.

I have a friend who is a constant interrupter. Whilst she is a lovely person, and is passionate and gets excited about particular topics, she does this in business conversations as well and in her hurry to dominate and get her knowledge out, she doesn't realise that she is disempowering herself in the dynamic of the relationship.

Others interrupt because they feel that they can help and they have the answers and they are excited to get it out, but again, it is about their desire to be heard, not to listen.

Do you find yourself constantly in arguments and conflicts? It could be because of your bad attitude in conversations.

A bad attitude can be a real conversation killer. It can make people feel uncomfortable, defensive, and uninterested in talking to you. If you find that you often have a bad attitude in conversations, it's time to make a change. Sometimes during mid life changes we can think and feel that we are communicating correctly but instead we are being seen as having a bad attitude.

Apart from being an interrupter, another sign of a bad attitude in conversation is being dismissive. When someone shares their thoughts or experiences with you, or a different opinion or perspective than you, don't immediately dismiss it or try to argue against it. Instead, try to understand where they're coming from and try to actively listen and engage with what they're saying and have a respectful discussion.

Take a breath in conversations. They are a two way street. Everyone wishes to be heard and understood and if you are in too much of a hurry to say your piece, then don't be surprised if it falls on deaf ears.

Assuming you know what someone else is thinking in a conversation can be a common mistake that many of us make. We might think we know what they're going to say, or assume we know how they're feeling, but this can lead to miscommunication and misunderstanding.

One sign that you're assuming you know what someone else is thinking is finishing their sentences. While it might seem like you're helping them out, finishing someone else's sentences can make them feel like you're not really listening to them. Instead of assuming what they're going to say, give them the opportunity to finish their own thoughts.

Another sign of assuming you know what someone else is thinking is not giving them a chance to speak. If you're constantly talking over them or interrupting them, you're not giving them a chance to share their own perspective. This can lead to misunderstandings and make the conversation feel one-sided.

Assuming you know what someone else is thinking can mean not asking questions. If you think you already know what someone else is thinking or feeling, you might not ask them questions to clarify. This can lead to miscommunication and leave both parties feeling frustrated.

It's important to be aware of our tone when we communicate with others, as it can greatly impact the effectiveness of our message and how it is received by the listener.

Tone refers to the way we use our voice to convey meaning and emotion when we speak. It is an important aspect of communication, as it can greatly influence the message we are trying to convey.
Tone can convey a range of emotions, from anger and frustration to joy and enthusiasm. It can also reveal underlying attitudes or intentions, such as sarcasm or condescension.

For example, if someone speaks in a harsh or angry tone, the listener may feel attacked or defensive, even if the words themselves are not necessarily negative. On the other hand, if someone speaks in a warm and friendly tone, the listener may feel more open and receptive to the message being conveyed.

Tone can also be influenced by nonverbal cues, such as facial expressions, body language, and gestures. These cues can reinforce the emotional message being conveyed and provide additional context for the listener.

Correcting someone about their tone in a conversation can be a difficult and delicate matter. While it may seem helpful to point out a negative tone or attitude, it can actually be counterproductive and create further tension and conflict in the conversation.

Correcting someone about their tone can come across as judgmental or confrontational, which can make the other person defensive and less receptive to what you have to say.

It can also shift the focus of the conversation away from the main point and onto the perceived negative tone or attitude, derailing the conversation and creating further misunderstandings.
Additionally, tone can be subjective and influenced by a range of factors, such as stress, fatigue, or emotions.

What one person perceives as a negative tone, another person may not. Correcting someone about their tone can therefore be based on a subjective interpretation and may not necessarily reflect the intent or meaning behind their words.

Furthermore, correcting someone about their tone can be seen as a personal attack, which can damage the relationship and trust between the two parties. It can also create a power dynamic in the conversation, where one person is seen as the authority on communication and the other as the inferior.

Instead of correcting someone about their tone, it's more effective to focus on the message being conveyed and address any misunderstandings or concerns directly. This can help to keep the conversation on track and avoid further conflict or tension.

It's natural to want to share your problems with the people closest to you, especially in a romantic relationship. After all, your partner is supposed to be there for you through thick and thin, right? However, it's important to remember that there's a difference between sharing your problems and off-loading them onto your partner.

Off-loading your problems onto your partner can put a strain on your relationship, as it creates a dynamic where your partner feels responsible for fixing your problems. This can lead to feelings of resentment and frustration on both sides.

Instead of off-loading your problems onto your partner, try to approach them as a team. Share your problems, but also come up with solutions together. This not only shows that you value your partner's input, but also takes some of the pressure off of them.

Remember, a healthy relationship is built on communication, trust, and mutual support. By approaching your problems as a team, you can strengthen your relationship and overcome any obstacle together.

Friends are a valuable source of support and comfort when we're going through tough times. But it's important to remember that off-loading your problems onto your friends can also put a strain on your friendship.

Constantly venting about your problems without taking any steps to solve them can make your friends feel drained and overwhelmed. Additionally, if you rely too heavily on your friends for emotional support, it can make them feel like they're not getting enough in return.

Instead of off-loading your problems onto your friends, try to approach them with a specific problem you're facing and ask for their input or advice. This shows that you value their opinion and are willing to work together to find a solution.

It's also important to make sure you're giving as much as you're getting in your friendships. Take the time to listen to your friends' problems and offer support when they need it.
Remember, healthy friendships are built on trust, mutual support, and open communication. By approaching your problems with your friends in a constructive way, you can strengthen your friendships and navigate life's challenges together.

Energy vampires are people who drain your energy and leave you feeling emotionally and mentally exhausted. They can be family members, friends, coworkers, or acquaintances who constantly complain, criticise, or demand attention without reciprocating or showing gratitude. Being around energy vampires can lead to feelings of stress, anxiety, and even physical exhaustion.

Energy vampires tend to have a negative outlook on life and complain frequently about their circumstances. They often demand attention, support, or validation without reciprocating or showing gratitude. This type of person tends to create or attract drama and chaos in their lives, which can be emotionally exhausting for those around them.

Energy vampires may be critical of others and make them feel inadequate or inferior.

Being around energy vampires can have a significant impact on your well-being and energy levels. However, there are ways to protect yourself from their draining effects, including: Setting clear boundaries and saying no to demands or requests that feel draining can help you protect your energy.

Limiting contact or reducing the amount of time spent with energy vampires can help you preserve your energy and reduce the impact of their draining effects. Surrounding yourself with positive, uplifting people can help counterbalance the negative effects of energy vampires.

Practicing self-care, such as exercising, meditating, or engaging in hobbies, can help you recharge your energy and reduce the impact of energy vampires.

Menopause

What is Menopause

Menopause is a natural part of the female aging process. Perimenopause and menopause are triggered by hormones that fluctuate and decrease. Every woman's experience is unique to them.

Perimenopause

this is the beginning stage of the physical changes during which a woman is making the transition to menopause. It can last up to ten years, starts on average in your mid forties and is basically the period during which your oestrogen levels start to drop and your ability to conceive diminishes. This is when you will start to observe symptoms like changes to your periods, hot flushes, sweating, disturbed sleep, painful joints, mood swings, weight gain, decreased sexual drive etc.

Menopause
You are at the next stage, classed a menopause, when you have not menstruated for a full 12 month cycle. The symptoms that you have in peri don't end they can become more severe. The average age of menopause is 51.

Post Menopause
Refers to the years after menopause, where the symptoms have slowly decreased over the years and your body is more acclimated to the lower levels of oestrogen.

You have to have a sense of humour about menopause or it will do your head in. It's this period of time, pun intended, where your periods are finally going to stop. From roughly the age of 45 a woman can be in the state of peri-menopause on your way to entering menopause when you haven't had a period for a year. You are going through some monumental changes in your physical and emotional self that mark the end of your fertile female journey, or basically babe, your eggs are running out.

We live in an ageist society and it's time to let women over fifty know that they can change their lives, they are not old, rather, age is a state of mind. Women age themselves out of life with their mental attitude. If you continually say to yourself I'm old, then you will be old, you will get old!

Our thoughts and our words are very powerful so if you can start making some changes in your personal self aging talk and be more aware of your thoughts and how they are often programmed into your everyday speech, by yourselves and others around you, including society, then maybe some blocks towards making some individual life changes will clear.

I believe women shouldn't feel that to be accepted into society and be perceived as beautiful, that they need to have unlined skin. I believe that a positive aging mindset is the most powerful aging gracefully tool that anyone needs.

Looking good in our skin is also about feeling good, so a healthy diet and regular exercise and drinking water are key as a healthy body on the inside, shows on the outside.

When you get to your fifties there are not many fashion ranges for us, not much advertising for the over fifties and pre and post-menopausal women can often feel invisible and overlooked, old and used up, coupled with often negative self talk.

Not surprising really, as this demographic is barely visually represented in mainstream fashion advertising. The women on the pages and covers of fashion magazines are heavily retouched, their pores are non- existent as is their facial hair and their wrinkles. In real life these women often don't look anything like their images, they are aliens!

Advertisers should be using the over 50's who look fabulous! And there are lots of you out there!

In Jungian philosophy, the archetypal female journey represented by maiden, mother, crone is outdated and was written in a time when humans did not live as long as we do now. In the olden days 1800's, life expectancy was 47.8 years and in the 1900's was 50. Where women would be grandmothers and old when they were in their 50's, hence the crone reference.

Today women often live healthy, physically fit lives well into their 90's. So there is a substantial difference between then and now and a huge gap in time where a fourth archetype already exists in modern society and this is the third stage, or Queen stage.

In some forms of feminist spirituality, the Maiden/Mother/Crone is used as an example of society's treatment of women. While the Maiden is revered and the Mother is honoured, the Crone is pushed aside and reviled. Women in their 50's and 60's today are vibrant, sexual, life-embracing women who are proud to be labeled as Queen, definitely not crone.

Instead of hiding in the shadows, they are reinventing themselves and stepping into their feminine power as they step into their pubapausal journey, doing deep internal work, dealing with their past using gratitude and forgiveness whilst moving through menopause from Mother to Queen. I hate the word crone and all that it envisages.

I believe that as we age, when we forgive our past and come to an understanding of who we are, we step fully into our healed selves and can move through our Queen stage, where for many it's their second prime of life. Blossoming into the Sage old woman, the wise revered one who is kind and caring. However, if we don't heal, we can become crones, bitter and resentful of our missed opportunities.

Some amazing women in society that we look up to today that are most definitely Queens and not crones are Oprah 68, Michelle Obama 58, Ellen 64, Madonna 64, J Lo 52

The Freudian interpretation of the Maiden/Mother/Crone appears in a variety of forms in film and television, although we may not always recognise it as such. They are the maiden (often blonde and beautiful, and either a naive ditz or a budding seductress), the mother, (often plump and rather eccentric, or pregnant), and the crone (often sharp witted, sharp tongued, bitter and unsentimental).

In terms of a Freudian trio, the maiden is the Id, the crone is the Superego, and the mother is the Ego. Even though they are the same being, they seem to know and think different things, so they "bicker." It's up to you to embrace your queen, not pay attention to your age number and the limitations that society wants to place on you and fully believe that age is just a number and you can do anything you set your mind to!

We are the elders of society, It's up to us to lead the younger generations. Start the conversation in society that aging is a good thing, that embracing our Queen and the life wisdom and knowledge we have acquired is a good thing and start embracing our wrinkles rather than be embarrassed by them.

HORMONE CHANGES

MANY PARTS OF THE BODY ARE AFFECTED AS OUR HORMONAL LEVELS FLUCTUATE AND DECLINE.

These include:

Reproductive system, Vaginal tract, Urinary system, Nervous system, Heart, Brain, Bones, Skin

Your menstrual cycle is regulated by the luteinizing hormone and follicle stimulating hormone. These two hormones are manufactured in the pituitary gland. They stimulate the ovaries to produce eastrogen and progesterone. During perimenopause and menopause these hormones fluctuate and can cause the following painful symptoms.

Cramps and Breast tenderness

Changes in your period may be accompanied by cramping that is more painful and intense than you were used to. You may also experience increased breast tenderness before and during menstruation. And you may find that your menstrual flow is light some months and heavy during others.

Migrane Headaches

Fluctuations in estrogen are linked to migraine headaches. You may get migraines for the first time or see an increase in severity or frequency during perimenopause. Some women have the reverse reaction, and see a reduction in migraine occurrence as they enter menopause. This may be because high levels of estrogen can trigger headaches and diminishing levels can cause a decrease.

Joint Pain

Menopause may cause joint pain that can affect the knees, shoulders, neck, elbows, or hands. Old joint injuries may begin to ache. As time goes on, you may start to notice that you feel more aches and pains in those areas than you used to. That's because estrogen helps to reduce inflammation. As it's levels decline, inflammation may increase, causing discomfort and menopause-related arthritis.

Pain During Intercourse

Pain can sometimes accompany sex when you're in menopause. This can make maintaining intimacy challenging. But women can find ways to keep their sex lives pleasurable during perimenopause, menopause and beyond. Estrogen the hormone which is in short supply during menopause, helps keep vaginal tissues elastic. It also supports moisture production in the vagina, which helps to make sex comfortable.

As estrogen levels recede, vaginal tissues get thinner. This can make intercourse painful. The vagina also becomes less lubricated, and more prone to inflammation, dryness, and tearing. Vaginal atrophy can also occur. This can cause the vagina to shrink and shorten in length.
Vaginal atrophy can be accompanied by urinary tract symptoms, such as: urinary leakage, burning during urination, urgent need to urinate.

Changes in hormone levels may also create a reduction in sexual desire, and a lessened ability to become sexually stimulated. This can make it even harder for the vagina to become lubricated.
These changes may happen at any point during perimenopause or menopause.

Bruising

The outside of the body is also affected by fluctuating and declining hormones. Low levels of oestrogen can cause a decrease in skins elasticity. It also lessens skins ability to retain water, which it uses as a buffer against injury.This makes skin thinner and painful bruising is often the result. You may also find that the elasticity in your skin is different now and you have knee wrinkles.

Hot Flashes

Hot flashes are the hallmark symptom of estrogen fluctuation, which occurs during the menopausal transition. A hot flash is generally characterised by a sudden sensation of intense body heat, often with profuse sweating of the head, neck, and chest. Hot flashes often occur at night, lasting several seconds to minutes, and can result in significant sleep deprivation.

Hot flashes may be accompanied by heart palpitations, anxiety, irritability, and panic. Although not life threatening, hot flashes can significantly impact a woman's quality of life, functional ability, sexuality, and self-image.

So many women want to manage their menopause symptoms as naturally as possible. Lifestyle and behavioural changes including diet, exercise, mind-body therapies, relaxation exercises and stress management are the foundation for effective movement through this transition phase, helping you to feel, think and perform at your best.

A decision to use supplements should be made in consultation with your physician, taking into account your individual health history and risks. This is not medical advice, but I hope this discussion will give women a starting point for those conversations with their physicians about natural therapies to improve their sleep, protect their health, and reduce their uncomfortable symptoms during menopause.

Hair Thinning

Hair loss tends to be subtler in women than in men, with women experiencing overall thinning rather than bald spots.
Hair may also fall out in clumps during brushing or showering. Directly related to a lowered production of estrogen and progesterone which are the hormones that help hair grow faster and stay on the head for longer periods of time.

When these levels drop, hair grows more slowly and can become much thinner. A decrease in these hormones also triggers an increase in the production of androgens, or a group of male hormones. Androgens shrink hair follicles, resulting in hair loss on the head. In some cases, however, these hormones can cause more hair to grow on the face. This is why some menopausal women develop facial "peach fuzz" and small sprouts of hair on the chin.

However, there are many other factors that can contribute to hair loss during menopause. These include extremely high levels of stress, illness, or a lack of certain nutrients. Diagnostic blood tests that can help rule out other causes of hair loss include thyroid tests, and/or a complete blood count.

Hair loss may make you feel self-conscious about your physical appearance, but the condition isn't permanent.

WOMEN.
SOMETIMES WE FEEL LIKE OUR ENERGY IS LIMITLESS!

We juggle life and we try to steal time to work on ourselves, our families, our jobs and then we realise that we do have limits, we don't have enough time for everyone, so we put ourselves last, we make choices and then we feel guilty as we can't spread ourselves around and be everything to everyone. Our feelings and emotions are all over the shop and we can feel irritable and depressed and be on a rollercoaster ride of emotions, some of which don't even feel like they make sense.

What is Happening??

As our hormone levels begin to decline in the months and years leading up to menopause, the hormone receptors in our brain begin running on empty. There is a disruption in an entire chain of biochemical activity which in turn affects the production of mood- regulating chemicals, including serotonin and endorphins. The end result can be mood swings, temper tantrums, anxiety, depression, highs and lows, brain fog or as I like to call it - menopause memory.

There are no shortcuts through menopause and we often find that we are pushing through this period of life, relying purely on the brute force of our personality. There is guilt and shame and confusion attached to not being yourself and not feeling great, so we hide it and push it all away and pretend that we are fine. That just leaves us feeling like crap.

Take a Deep Breath
There are going to be times in this part of your life journey when you are going to have some full-on mood swings. You are going to completely misread a situation, a conversation or a moment with people close to you, because that's what happens when our brain chemistry is a bit out of whack.

Whenever you do get really angry and find your emotions are all rushing to the surface and you are getting upset, take a deep breath, step back and let a little time pass - counting to ten in your head works. You need to include all your conversations, whether via text or email, in person, on the phone or social media comments, just do yourself a favour and take a breath and pause before you reply. It is so easy to get triggered, lash out and lose friends.

Chances are when the mood swing passes, as it always does, you may be glad you didn't lash out at someone who may not deserve it.
However, if the mood passes and you still feel the same way, then by all means do what you must to clear the air. While many problems can temporarily seem bigger than they are during this time of life, real problems can also occur. But taking a little time between action and reaction may be all you need to do, to know the difference.

THINGS MAY GET WEIRD

Caring communication and understanding between both you and your husband or your significant other about the changes your body is going through is really important.

You both need to be on board for this part of your life journey together as things may get a little weird. It takes years whilst you are in perimenopause for your body to wind down and run out of eggs and all the visual changes are things we can see, like hot sweats. But there are insidious things that can happen to our bodies when our hormones become out of balance.

Our moods are affected, our memory, our skin, our sleep, our joints can ache and our muscles can feel sore and weak. Then all of a sudden you are in menopause and your hormones have depleted and you can have some full on uncontrollable mood swings. Complete understanding of your body by both of you is really important as support from your husband and family is vital at this stage.

Understanding that you can have heightened emotional responses to situations, because of your out of whack hormones, including all the other stuff, helps your husband give you the emotional, physical, mental support and understanding that you may need at this time.

Get your husband involved from the beginning, get him googling info so he understands that your journey is something you must not do alone without understanding and support from him.

There can be serious complications to your hormones depleting like fractured bones and your personality and your zest for life can completely change to the point of losing yourself mentally so caring communication is the key.

It's a fact that more women in their fifties go through divorce than any other age. Is this because of miscommunication and misunderstanding of menopause by their husbands and partners...I have often wondered.

It is a fact that women frequently use alternative medicine treatments to manage menopause. Like natural products - such as soy and herbal remedies, mind body practices - including yoga and meditation and traditional Chinese medicine - including acupuncture and herbs. Women often try more natural ways to treat menopausal symptoms because they often feel that biomedical treatments like HRT (Hormone Replacement Therapy) and bio-identical hormones as treatments are too aggressive. My advice on having bones fracture because of menopause, is never say never.

However, every woman's journey is a unique one and you may have done lots of research on what you will and will not take, because of the side effects mentioned and the risks involved. However, you must make space for changes in your treatment to occur and be open to suggestions for the more medical route, depending on the severity of your symptoms.

Always communicate with your doctor as to what natural remedies and treatments you have been using as some herbs are very powerful and may have contraindications when used with HRT.

During this time I have found that dealing with a female GP, who has experience with menopause, preferably her own, is going to make for a much better communication journey. Nothing against male doctors or young doctors in general but when you are menopausal there is a part of your emotional brain that's not interested in listening to an inexperienced Dr or one who doesn't listen.

Being told by a male anyone to lose weight when you are sweaty and menopausal just triggers you into unpleasant feelings, so it's best to find a female specialist.

When women are experiencing mood swings and other challenges of menopause your husband or partner may not know how to support you. "I just feel wrong no matter what I do or say." Your partner has to realise that it's not personal but that sometimes you are going to feel like shit and your emotions may be in a negative space.

That sometimes you may feel that you lack sex appeal and are old, unattractive, or dispensable. The physical changes you endure during this time may cause weakness, forgetfulness, or discomfort and you may feel sad or angry as you enter a new stage of life. This is a time in your relationship where fine-tuning your relationship skills is going to come in handy.

However, not all menopausal women have mood swings and they embrace it all feeling strong, happy or hopeful. They may also feel that their life experiences have made them wise, competent and indispensable. Often you will feel like you are getting your second wind and are ready to embrace change. If you are in good health and have looked after your physical self by being aware of your diet and exercise, then you may be happy that you are looking great as you age.

At the same time as you are menopausal there are many other areas of your health to keep an eye on. It is important to keep up cervical screening and breast checks and to watch your diet, blood pressure and cholesterol to ensure good cardiovascular health. Lower levels of oestrogen also increase the risk of bladder weakness and osteoporosis.

You need your own space babe

You're married and you've been with hubby for quite a few years and I know you've been sleeping together and sharing the same bed forever and you are both in the habit of doing it, it feels weird if you don't sleep together that sounds like too radical a change.

But when you are sleeping with the air conditioner on, pumping it out at 20 degrees in the middle of winter, separating your sleeping arrangements, into separate bedrooms if possible, will save your marriage and your sanity. Let's face it, being woken by giant farts or loud snoring or sleep talking is not romantic for you or him.

You may need your own space, as night sweats, temperature changes, sleepless nights, different sleep patterns, aggravation at a snoring partner, or snoring yourself. Feeling guilty if you wake him up and vice versa. During this time your sleep cycle is going to be disturbed and it's going to be erratic for ages, maybe years. So If it's possible for you to have your own bed and sleep alone, it will improve your quality of life.

Both of you will sleep better and it's important for you both to have your separate alone times, more personal freedom is healthy in a long term relationship.
Get a tv watch stuff at night, podcasts, educational stuff, etc. Learning absorbing growing in the comfort of your own private space, having meditative time with your thoughts. It's time to reclaim control of the remote.

Coming together for sex and date nights, but not spending the night sleeping together, makes intimacy more sacred and special.

Sexual space

One of the key symptoms of menopause is a dry vagina. Lower levels of oestrogen directly affect your vagina and can make the skin thinner, dryer and less elastic. Testosterone levels fall gradually with age and this can have an impact on your sexual function and libido.

Coupled with lack of sleep, hit flushes and fatigue makes it less likely you will be as interested in having sex. Some women are concerned with their lack of libido and feel they have lost that sexy feeling and others are not so worried.

It really depends on you, your attitude to sex, your age, how menopause has affected you, your relationship, whether you want to have sex and all the other things that may be going on with your life at the time. Caring communication with your husband to let him know that you are just not feeling it and why, will help him to understand the physical sexual changes.

Lubrication like sylk can be used and some women use coconut oil, however if you have vaginal atrophy and the walls are thin, then sex can be very uncomfortable and hurt, even causing tearing and abrasions, so penetration of anything during this stage, feels just not worth it.

Hormone therapy for the vagina called vagifem is a popular estrogen therapy in pessary form and it is helpful in the post menopausal stage to strengthen the internal vaginal walls.

Space and time

Make space in your busy life for yourself. For a walk, a stretch, a read, a watch or a listen of something just for you. You will need the time to rest, taking a break and having an hour or so to just be with yourself and have some alone time, is going to be necessary.

Date space

Your sexual relationship with your partner and your feelings about your physical self may change, so having time together with your man when he's putting you first and nurturing you, is important to your relationship.
If hubby is not on board with the changes you are going through you may find yourselves growing distant over the years and you may resent him for not being more involved. Stay connected with each other.

Date Nights

Make time for date nights if you don't already. Chat with your partner about your intimate future. If you have been in a relationship for a long time and you are open to it, role playing is fun. My husband had his alter ego Jai, the Brazilian massage therapist. Jai talks in an accent, wears beads and hippy shorts, arrives with a portable massage bed and is there to service me with a lovely full body massage that often comes with a happy ending…just for me!

Subconscious space

You will have psychological baggage and moments from your past, that you have held onto from your pubescent years. We all do. Things that have happened to you that have shaped the woman that you are today and these moments and experiences are taking up space in your subconscious.

This period in your female development is your pubapausal time where you need to revisit your past and start digging deep into your wounds to learn by them and heal from them. This process of deep healing and learning forgiveness for self and others, is one of the key elements into transforming yourself into your true authentic self and reaching your full potential as the one in a trillion unique females on our planet.

It can feel challenging for some women to realise that their fertile period is coming to an end. And for some they feel like they are getting old or over the hill in their 50's however, that is so far from the truth. You are coming out of your fertile maiden and mother archetypal phase and transforming into your queen stage when you are in menopause.

It's a wonderful, exciting feeling to come out the other side of this journey having reunited your heart, reframed your mind and redesigned your spirit for the next half of your existence.

There is an end to menopause symptoms and you will come out the other side feeling fine. This will however go on for many years and changes in your life need to be made to support yourself.

Manifestation and Gratitude

Manifestation and gratitude go hand in hand as far as I'm concerned. I really feel that I manifested my win as Mrs Earth Australia. I did not let my age hold me back at all and refused to have any doubt whatsoever that I could do it. I would speak about it to others as if it was already a given, not if I win but when I win. And not in an arrogant way because I would preface that with I'm manifesting my win.

I held it in my heart and in my head and had faith that I could do it. I also filled myself up with gratitude to the universe for delivering it to me. However, you need to be prepared to receive what your heart desires. You need to be ready to receive and show the universe that you are proactive.

I remember reading a story about manifesting and there was a part where a woman was ready to have a man in her life, she really wanted a boyfriend. However her actions in life were not showing that she was prepared to receive. Her wardrobe was full of her clothes, she parked in the middle of her garage, she slept in the middle of her bed.

So one day she made room in her life to receive her new partner. She made space in her wardrobe for someone else to put their clothes, she started sleeping on one side of the bed and parking on one side of the garage and before she knew it, her new partner arrived in her life.

Just like I practised walking in high heeled shoes and wore dresses and I immersed myself online into the pageant world and I learnt about it and what was expected of me and I practised walking and studied online. I got training from an international coach on how to do my speech and how to represent myself in the interview section. I worked hard, I did my homework on this new industry that I was getting ready to enter. I prepared to receive. I practised gratitude everyday in my life for everything I had and all that I was.

Like those people that wish to win the lottery, you've at least got to buy a ticket! If you haven't either watched or read the secret by Rhonda Byrne, I suggest you do.
Manifestation is also deeply connected to the words you use and speak out loud. I had a friend who would loudly declare upon entering a car perk that she never got a parking space, this was her mantra when ever she arrived. Do you think she ever got one, well no, because she had declared it so.

I on the other hand always get a car space and it's always close to where I need to be. I believe it is waiting for me, I believe it will manifest for me and I always get one, regardless of where I am. It's all about what you believe you receive.

When we were little, playing make believe games was something we were excellent at. We would immerse ourselves into our imaginary worlds and stay there for hours, fully believing in the world we had created for ourselves.

Manifestation is playing make believe. Making it all up in your head, what ever you wish to receive or achieve and believing with all your heart that you have already received it.

The universe doesn't understand time, so if you are saying thanks I would like that next week or next month, the energetic frequency you are giving out won't really work. You have to be on the frequency of having already received it, this is really important. If you have already received something then your energy and your gratitude is going to be so much bigger than if you want something that you haven't got, right? So always make it past tense in your head and your heart and you will be on the right energetic frequency to manifest.

You will also receive it when you are ready. The universe doesn't respond to demands with time attached so be mindful of your thoughts at all times.

Practising gratitude involves being happy and saying thank you. Thank you to the universe or God. Thank you for all that you have in your life, all those that are in it. Your physical self, nature and your surroundings. Gratitude is the attitude for altitude. If you find it difficult to feel gratitude then try starting small, like being grateful that you woke up.

First thing you do when you wake up is smile and say thank you.
Write in a journal of things you can be grateful for and have it sitting by your bed so it is close. Your friends, your family, your health, your wealth. Just start writing down 30 things you are grateful for, starting with I Am. Then keep going and read them every day as a reminder of all the good things in your life, even if you are not in a great situation.

My favourite Disney movie when I was growing up was Pollyanna, she would always play the Glad Game, finding the good in every day even though her life wasn't as happy as it could have been. She put herself in a joy state all the time and this is something I have practised my whole life.

I'm one of those happy people that always sees the good and the positive in every situation, regardless of what it may be.

At the end of each day, write in your journal what you are gratful for in that day, you will start to see the little things in life that all add up to the bigger moments. You will start to be more mindful of the world around you, which leads to practising mind mastery.

Having faith in yourself means having confidence and trust in your abilities, character, and judgment. It's about believing in yourself and your potential to succeed, even in the face of challenges and setbacks. When you have faith in yourself, you're able to take risks, pursue your goals, and overcome obstacles with resilience and determination.

When you have faith in yourself, you believe that you have the skills, knowledge, and talents necessary to succeed in your endeavours. You recognise your strengths and weaknesses and have confidence in your ability to learn and grow.

Having faith in yourself also means trusting your instincts and making decisions based on your own values and beliefs. You're able to weigh the pros and cons of a situation and make choices that align with your goals and aspirations.

When you have faith in yourself, you believe in your own integrity, honesty, and moral principles. You're able to stand up for what you believe in and make decisions that are in line with your values. Having faith in yourself also involves the ability to bounce back from setbacks and challenges. You're able to persevere in the face of adversity, and you don't give up on your goals or aspirations.

Having faith in yourself is essential for personal growth, development, and success. It allows you to take risks, pursue your passions, and achieve your goals with confidence and determination. When you have faith in yourself, you're able to overcome self-doubt and insecurity, and you're able to face challenges with resilience and optimism.

You can also have faith in a higher being, which is where religion and having faith can be intertwined.

Spirituality is a broad term that refers to the quest for meaning and purpose in life. It encompasses a wide range of beliefs, practices, and experiences related to the human spirit or soul. Spirituality is often associated with religious or mystical experiences, but it can also be a deeply personal and individual journey.

We are all spiritual beings having a human experience inside a human form. I believe that we are all connected and that is a beautiful and magical energetic consciousness.

At its core, spirituality involves a sense of connection to something greater than oneself. This can be a higher power, a universal consciousness, nature, or humanity as a whole. Spirituality often involves a search for answers to the big questions of life, such as the meaning of existence, the nature of reality, and the purpose of human suffering.

Spirituality can take many different forms. For some people, it involves following a specific religious tradition and participating in organised worship, prayer, or meditation. For others, it may involve exploring alternative spiritual practices such as yoga, mindfulness, or shamanism.
Some people may find spirituality through creative expression, such as music, art, or writing, while others may find it through community service or activism.

Spirituality can have a profound impact on a person's life. It can provide a sense of purpose and direction, foster a sense of inner peace and well-being, and help people cope with life's challenges and difficulties. It can also help people connect with others and build supportive communities.

While spirituality is often associated with religion, it's important to note that spirituality can also be a deeply personal and individual journey. People from all walks of life and all belief systems can experience spirituality in their own unique way.

Daily Disciplines

In this chapter you will find 6 daily disciplines that are healthy to embrace to disrupt the aging process within you. These work on all four holistic pillars that hold us up, mental, emotional, physical and spiritual.

As we forge ahead on our mission to redefine aging and mid-life, it's time to discuss the essential role self-discipline plays in our journey. Embracing self-discipline enables us to defy age, preserve our vitality, and flourish both physically and mentally, even in the face of demanding daily lives. Let's delve deeper into how self-discipline can empower us to become true Aging Disrupters.

To kick-start your journey to self-discipline, begin by setting achievable goals that align with your Aging Disrupter mission. Start with small steps and progressively build on them. In our Move It or Lose It program, for instance, we initiate a daily routine such as walking for 30 minutes. As you gain confidence and embrace your Aging Disrupter mindset, you can gradually increase the intensity and duration of your workouts.

You can add to your physical workout by embracing some of the exercise modalities mentioned in chapter nine and choose those that resonate with you.

Create a schedule to prioritise your commitments, treating them as essential appointments. Allocate time in your calendar for body activation workouts, preferably in the morning before your busy day begins. Hold yourself accountable to that schedule, knowing that doing so supports your mission to redefine the aging process.

Start training yourself to be an early riser if you are not already and go for a walk at the very start of the day before everyone else is awake. I love to meditate whilst I am walking and think about all the things I am grateful for, whilst walking with my dog in a beautiful park. I love starting my day like this and have made it a habit that I miss when I don't do. By honouring your commitments, you're not only investing in your physical health but also nourishing your mind and soul.

Cultivating discipline in all areas of your life be it your exercise schedule, what you eat or what you think, requires patience and effort. If you falter, don't abandon your journey. Instead, view setbacks as opportunities to learn, grow, and reaffirm your commitment to your goals. Remember that resilience is a hallmark of true Aging Disrupters, who know that perseverance will lead to a healthier, more vibrant life.

HABITS

Habits are automatic behaviours that we engage in without conscious thought. They can be positive or negative, and they can have a significant impact on our daily lives. Forming new habits can be challenging, but it's worth the effort if it means improving our health, productivity, or overall well-being.

So, how long does it take to form a habit? The answer can vary depending on the individual and the habit in question. Some experts say it takes 21 days to form a new habit, while others suggest it can take anywhere from 18 to 254 days, depending on the person and the habit.

The truth is, forming a new habit requires consistent effort and repetition. It's not enough to simply do something once or twice and expect it to become a habit overnight. You need to commit to the habit for an extended period and make it a regular part of your routine.

Here are some tips for forming new habits:

1. Start small. Don't try to tackle too much at once. Focus on one habit at a time and start with a small, achievable goal.
2. Be consistent. Try to practice your new habit at the same time every day or on the same days of the week.
3. Track your progress. Keep a record of your progress to help you stay motivated and accountable.
4. Be patient. It may take several weeks or even months to form a new habit. Don't give up if you don't see results right away.
5. Reward yourself. Celebrate your successes along the way and give yourself a pat on the back for sticking with your new habit.

1. SELF LOVE

Self-love is the act of caring for yourself physically, emotionally, and mentally. It's about accepting yourself for who you are and recognising your own worth. Self-love is essential because it helps you maintain a positive relationship with yourself, which is the foundation for healthy relationships with others.

Self-love involves taking care of your basic needs such as getting enough sleep, eating a balanced diet, exercising regularly, and practicing good hygiene. It also involves taking care of your emotional well-being by acknowledging and expressing your feelings, setting boundaries, and engaging in activities that bring you joy.

Practicing self-love means being kind and gentle with yourself, forgiving yourself for mistakes, and treating yourself with compassion. It involves recognising your strengths and celebrating your accomplishments, no matter how small they may be. Self-love also means learning from your failures and using them as opportunities for growth.

Self-love requires a commitment to yourself and your well-being. It's not always easy, and it may take time to develop. However, the benefits of self-love are immeasurable. When you love and care for yourself, you're more resilient, confident, and better equipped to handle life's challenges.

2. DRINKING WATER

Drinking 2 litres of filtered water a day is so important for an aging body, good for joints, and reducing dehydration in the skin. If you don't already do this, it needs to be the number one thing you do.
Get into the habit of drinking a big glass of water as soon as you wake up. I have mine in a special glass as well that holds over 500ml, so it has become a routine that I do whilst the kettle boils for my first cuppa of the day.

When I wasn't drinking at least two litres a day, not only had a developed wrinkles on my face, but on my arms and legs as well. I promise you that when you increase your intake of water substantially, you will see the benefits in the skin on your entire body.

As we age, it's important to prioritise our health and wellness to ensure that we maintain our vitality and energy. One key aspect of this is staying hydrated, and drinking 2 litres of filtered water a day can provide a range of benefits for our bodies. I bought an on the bench water filter model that alkalises my water and it tastes delicious.

Firstly, drinking enough water is important for maintaining healthy joints. Our joints are surrounded by synovial fluid, which acts as a cushion and lubricant to help protect our bones and prevent friction. When we're dehydrated, this fluid can become depleted, leading to increased stiffness, pain, and discomfort.

By drinking 2 litres of filtered water a day, we can help keep our joints healthy and lubricated, reducing the risk of injury and discomfort.
In addition to supporting healthy joints, drinking enough water is also important for reducing dehydration in the skin. As we age, our skin becomes thinner and more prone to dehydration, which can lead to a range of issues like dryness, flakiness, and premature aging.

Water can help keep our skin hydrated and plump, reducing the appearance of fine lines and wrinkles and promoting a more youthful, radiant complexion. I can guarantee that if you substantially increase your internal moisturising by increasing your water intake, those fine lines on your face, which are not aging lines but signs of skin dehydration, will disappear.

3. SKIN CARE

Taking care of our skin is an essential part of maintaining a youthful and healthy appearance as we age. A crucial daily discipline in any skincare routine is moisturising, which helps to prevent dryness, flakiness, and irritation while promoting a radiant complexion.

Daily moisturising on our face and body is vital because it helps to keep the skin looking youthful and healthy. Moisturisers work by trapping water in the skin, helping to prevent dryness and dehydration. As we age, our skin becomes less able to retain moisture on its own, making regular moisturising even more important.

Regular moisturising can help to reduce the appearance of fine lines and wrinkles, as well as prevent new ones from forming. When the skin is well hydrated, it is more elastic and plump, which can help to minimise the appearance of wrinkles and give the skin a more youthful glow.

In addition to its anti-aging benefits, moisturising can also help to improve the overall health and function of the skin. It can help to strengthen the skin's natural barrier, protecting it from environmental stressors such as pollution, UV rays, and harsh weather conditions.

Choose one that is right for your skin. You don't have to go for the expensive brands with the fancy packaging. You can also get samples from the larger makeup stores like Mecca and larger pharmacies to try and see how your skin agrees with them. Many also have a sunscreen added and I personally prefer to use those without sunscreen.

I love using oils on my skin as well as my usual go to moisturisers and find that castor oil, which is thick and full of omegas is an awesome oil for your face, as are the lighter textured oils of macadamia, argon, reship, jojoba and almond. Leave them on to soak in at night though, as they are not suitable for putting foundation over.

To maximise the benefits of your skincare routine, consider the following tips:
1. Cleanse your skin daily to remove dirt, oil, and makeup.
2. Exfoliate regularly to remove dead skin cells and promote cell turnover.
3. Apply sunscreen daily, even on cloudy days, to protect your skin from harmful UV rays.
4. Use products containing antioxidants, such as vitamin C, to help combat free radicals and environmental damage.
5. Be gentle with your skin, avoiding harsh scrubs or over-cleansing.

4. GRATITUDE

Practising daily gratitude is so good for both our mental and physical well-being. Every morning I start my day by saying thank you to the universe for all I have and all I am. I have a routine that I do every morning whilst the kettle is boiling for my first cup of tea.

I go outside and breathe deeply into my stomach and I appreciate the day before me. I then have a daily mantra that I say to start me off. This was taught to me by one of my coaches along my life path, James.

Thank you for my blessed life.

Thank you for this magnificent universe and thank you for this beautiful new day. Please bless all living things today with your love, your grace and your abundance. Please flow to me and through me, infinite love, joy, peace, purpose and prosperity.

I then thank the universe for all I wish to receive as if it has already happened. I visualise these things or moments and I send blessings out to the universe for friends and loved ones who may not be doing so well with their health.

I then have my big glass of water 500 mls and do my body activation exercises, which I teach as part of my course 60 is the new 40 the 30 day disrupt aging challenge.

I'm awake, full of gratitude and in a joy state to start my day and take my dog for her walk.

Focusing on what we're grateful for can help shift our perspective away from negative thoughts and emotions, leading to an overall boost in happiness and well-being.

Don't ever go to bed on an argument or feeling negative things about yourself or others or you will wake up with it. sort it out and move past it before you go to sleep or it will fester overnight, affecting your quality of sleep and your mind.

Also don't have angry sex with your partner, as we transfer our energies into another during the act of love making. It's called making love for a reason. I had a 30 year relationship with my husband and this was a credo I lived by. Quality over quantity is also the best sex to have.

Gratitude has been shown to help reduce stress and anxiety by promoting positive emotions and helping us cope with difficult situations. Expressing gratitude towards others can help strengthen relationships and foster feelings of connection and empathy.

Being in a state of gratitude can help us build resilience by providing a positive perspective on challenging situations and encouraging us to focus on our strengths and resources.

Studies have shown that practicing gratitude can have physical health benefits, such as improved sleep quality, reduced inflammation, and lowered blood pressure.

Practicing gratitude can take many forms, from keeping a daily gratitude journal to simply taking a few minutes each day to reflect on what we're thankful for. It's important to cultivate a sense of gratitude in a way that feels authentic and meaningful to us, whether through meditation, prayer, or other practices.

By incorporating gratitude into our daily lives, we can cultivate a sense of joy, positivity, and well-being that can have lasting effects on our mental and physical health.

5. POSTURE

Posture refers to the position of your body and the alignment of your bones, muscles, and joints. Good posture means that your body is properly aligned and balanced, which allows you to move and function more efficiently and effectively. On the other hand, poor posture can cause a range of problems, from discomfort and pain to more serious health issues.

When I was young the saying was, Stomach in, Shoulders back, Chest out, which was a reminder to activate those parts of your body to stand straight and have good posture. Breasts are often heavy and can cause us to slouch forwards putting strain and tension on our necks and upper back and leading to us hunching over.

Seated work at a desk in can also cause us to slouch our shoulders, which is why we now have ergonomic chairs to use for computer work, that encourage better posture to alleviate back and neck pain and weakness.

Holding your shoulders back and being body aware by practising good posture, distributes the weight of your body evenly across your muscles and joints, reducing the strain on any one area. This helps prevent muscle tension and soreness.

Good posture allows your lungs and diaphragm to work more efficiently, which means you can breathe more deeply and take in more oxygen. It also improves circulation, which delivers more oxygen and nutrients to your muscles and organs.

Good posture helps your digestive system function properly by allowing your internal organs to sit in their natural position. This can help prevent issues like acid reflux and constipation.

When you have good posture, your body is able to use its energy more efficiently. This can help you feel more alert and focused, and improve your productivity throughout the day.

Poor posture can cause a range of problems, from back and neck pain to headaches and joint pain. By maintaining good posture, you can reduce your risk of these issues and prevent discomfort and pain.

Be aware of your body alignment and start your daily discipline of having good posture. Remember, stomach in, shoulders back, chest out!
Much better than stomach out, shoulders slouched and breasts down.

6. SKIN DAILY DISCIPLINES - COLD SHOWER RINSES

While hot showers can feel soothing and relaxing, they can actually be detrimental to the health of your skin. Here are some reasons why:

1. Strips Natural Oils: Hot water can strip the skin of its natural oils, which are essential for keeping it hydrated and healthy. Without these oils, the skin can become dry, itchy, and prone to irritation.

2. Damages Skin Barrier: Hot water can also damage the skin's protective barrier, making it more susceptible to environmental pollutants and bacteria. This can lead to inflammation and breakouts.

3. Increases Redness: Hot water can cause blood vessels in the skin to dilate, leading to increased redness and irritation. This can be particularly problematic for people with sensitive skin or conditions like rosacea.

4. Aggravates Eczema and Psoriasis: Hot water can exacerbate conditions like eczema and psoriasis, causing them to flare up and become more painful and itchy.

5. Accelerates Aging: Hot water can cause premature aging by breaking down collagen and elastin fibres in the skin. This can lead to wrinkles, sagging, and a loss of firmness.

Taking a cold shower rinse may not sound like the most pleasant experience, but it can actually offer a wide range of health benefits. Here are some of the top benefits of taking cold shower rinses:

1. Boosts Circulation: Cold water can help to improve blood flow throughout the body. This can help to reduce inflammation, improve cardiovascular health, and enhance overall circulation.
2. Relieves Sore Muscles: Cold water can also help to reduce muscle soreness and stiffness. After a workout or physical activity, taking a cold shower rinse can help to ease sore muscles and reduce inflammation.
3. Increases Alertness: Taking a cold shower rinse can help to increase alertness and mental clarity. The shock of cold water can stimulate the body and wake up the mind, leading to improved focus and productivity.
4. Boosts Immune System: Cold water exposure has been shown to increase the production of white blood cells, which are important for fighting off infections and boosting the immune system.
5. Improves Skin and Hair Health: Cold water can help to improve skin and hair health by reducing inflammation and stimulating circulation. It can also help to reduce oil production in the skin, leading to a clearer complexion.
6. Reduces Stress and Anxiety: Cold water exposure has been shown to reduce levels of stress and anxiety. The shock of cold water can trigger the release of endorphins, which are natural mood-boosters.

Have your usual warm shower and finish it off with a cold shower rinse. If you are washing your hair let the jets hit your head first, then your back where the major organs are. Move round to your chest and the front of your body and your temperature will regulate pretty quickly.

I have been doing this for years, so much so that I don't feel refreshed or that I've had a proper shower with out the cold water rinse.

I feel it is one of the reasons that my skin has stayed firm and youthful looking and my hair is shiny and soft.

You won't be cold afterwards as your body will be working hard to warm your self up. It's a stimulating and refreshing way to rejuvenate your body and hair as an aging disrupter.

Mind Mastery

WHAT DOES MIND MASTERY MEAN?

Mind mastery is the practice of developing a greater awareness of our thoughts and emotions, and learning how to control them in order to achieve greater mental clarity, focus, and emotional well-being. It involves understanding the workings of the mind and learning how to use its power to achieve our goals and live a more fulfilling life.

Mindfulness has its roots in Buddhist meditation practices, but it has gained widespread popularity as a secular practice in recent years. It involves developing a non-judgmental and non-reactive awareness of our thoughts, feelings, and physical sensations, and accepting them without getting caught up in them.

At its core, mind mastery is about taking control of our thoughts and emotions, rather than letting them control us. It involves cultivating a greater sense of self-awareness, and learning how to identify and manage negative thought patterns and emotions that can hold us back from achieving our full potential.

Mind mastery also involves developing the ability to focus our attention on the present moment, rather than being distracted by worries about the past or future. This can help us cultivate greater clarity and focus in our work and personal lives, and lead to a greater sense of inner peace and well-being.

Practicing mindfulness can help us to reduce stress and anxiety, improve focus and concentration, and enhance our overall well-being. It can also help us to develop a greater sense of self-awareness and empathy towards others, which can improve our relationships and social interactions.

There are many practices and techniques that can be used to develop mind mastery, including meditation, mindfulness, visualisation, and positive affirmations. These practices can help us cultivate a greater sense of self-awareness and control over our thoughts and emotions, and can lead to greater success in our personal and professional lives.

At this mid life stage of our lives, its important to work on mastering our minds, as it is often, when we go through midlife, that things in our past that we may not have dealt with, will come to the surface and need to be sorted out. Being mindful of how we are thinking about ourselves in these moments will help us come to terms with our past which can often be childhood trauma and navigate our present and future selves with grace and forgiveness.

CONFIDENCE AND SELF ESTEEM ARE DIFFERENT

Confidence and self-esteem are two terms that are often used interchangeably, but they actually refer to different aspects of our sense of self. You can fake having confidence, but you can't fake having self-esteem.

Confidence refers to our belief in our ability to perform a specific task or achieve a specific goal. It's about feeling capable and competent in a particular area. Confidence can be situational, meaning we may feel confident in one area of our life but not in another. For example, we may feel confident in our ability to play a sport, but not in our ability to speak in public.

Self-esteem refers to our overall sense of worth and value as a person. It's about how we feel about ourselves in general, regardless of our abilities or achievements. Self-esteem is a more stable and enduring aspect of our sense of self. It can affect how we view ourselves and how we interact with the world around us.

It's possible to have high confidence in one area of our life but low self-esteem overall, or vice versa.

Having a healthy level of both confidence and self-esteem is important for our overall balance in our well-being. Confidence can help us achieve our goals and pursue our passions, while self-esteem can help us feel good about ourselves and navigate life's challenges with resilience and self-compassion.

HOW TO BUILD YOUR CONFIDENCE

Confidence is a crucial trait for success and personal growth. It allows you to take risks, pursue your goals, and overcome challenges with resilience and determination. However, building confidence is not always easy, and it can take time and effort.
Here are some tips on how to build more confidence:

Identify your strengths: One of the best ways to build confidence is to focus on your strengths. Make a list of your skills, talents, and accomplishments, and remind yourself of them regularly. Celebrate your successes and acknowledge your achievements.

Practice self-care: Taking care of yourself can help boost your confidence. This includes getting enough sleep, eating well, and exercising regularly. Taking care of your physical and mental health can help you feel more energised and confident.

Set achievable goals: Setting goals that are challenging yet achievable can help build your confidence. Break your goals into small, manageable steps, and celebrate your progress along the way.

Take on challenges: Facing challenges and stepping out of your comfort zone can help build confidence. Start with small challenges and gradually work your way up to bigger ones. Take risks and embrace new experiences.

Surround yourself with positive people: Surrounding yourself with supportive and positive people can help build your confidence. Seek out friends, mentors, and colleagues who believe in you and encourage you to pursue your goals.

Practice self-compassion: It's important to be kind and compassionate to yourself, especially when you make mistakes or experience setbacks. Instead of beating yourself up, practice self-compassion and remind yourself that everyone makes mistakes. If we don't fail at something, we will never learn how to be better.

Focus on the present: Focusing on the present moment and letting go of worries about the future or regrets about the past can help build confidence. Be mindful of your thoughts and emotions, and practice staying present in the moment. Living in the past and speaking about the past as if it is your present state of being will not help you build your confidence. Instead it will hinder your growth.

Be mindful of the words you use to describe yourself, in your head or outloud. We are what we think.

One way I love to help people build their confidence is through singing karaoke. When you get up there for the first time and your hand is shaking, and your tummy is full of butterflies, you are outside of your comfort zone. The beautiful thing about karaoke is that no one cares if you can really sing, that's the whole point.

The challenge is about giving it a go, pushing through the nerves. After you have made it through that first song, your adrenaline will be through the roof and your confidence will be soaring and you will be excited to find another song and do it al again!

HOW TO BUILD YOUR SELF ESTEEM

Low self esteem can impact all areas of your life, from personal relationships to business. It can be debilitating to have low self esteem and often body issues and how we feel about what we look like are a big part of this.

It's important to recognise situations that seem to deflate your self esteem. If you suffer from this, you know what they are. It's really helpful to have a coach in these situations to help you find yourself and all the positive in you if you can't yourself.

Write them down and take a look at them as they can be triggered by situations or people in our lives. Sometimes our relationships with those close to us can be disempowering and lead to us feeling lower than we should. This then is more about the other person and how they communicate with us, rather than ourselves.

Sometimes a trigger can be associated with work, which may involve speaking in public or making a presentation where we can sometimes doubt ourselves and the message we wish to convey.

Once you have written them down, you need to become aware of how you think about your self and the words you use to describe yourself. Are they positive, negative or neutral? Are they rational or are they based on false ideas? Ask your self if you would say these thoughts outloud to a friend to describe yourself to them. Would they see you as you see yourself in this moment?

Negative self talk is where you undervalue yourself or put yourself down. Jumping to negative conclusions about people, without knowing the facts is also detrimental to our emotional health. Social media is a great example of this. When you see someone has read your message but they don't reply straight away, then you may jump to a negative thought or judgement as to why they haven't. Without knowing what they are doing in their lives, or what their thoughts are. assuming that people think the worst about you is mind reading, no-one can do that.

I have a friend who would always reply when asked how he was with, " doing ok for an old bloke" this meant that he was only ok and that he was old. In fact he is 10 years younger than me. When I pointed out to him that his daily mantra was actually aging him, he stopped straight away.

So exercise mind mastery, be careful of the words you use to describe yourself and the thoughts you have. Switch them to more positive affirmations and you will elevate your self esteem and the mastery of your mind.

MINDSET - NEGATIVE

Being in a negative mindset means having a pessimistic and self-defeating attitude towards life. It's characterised by negative thoughts, feelings, and beliefs that can lead to a sense of hopelessness, anxiety, and depression.

When we're in a negative mindset, we tend to focus on the negative aspects of our lives and overlook the positive. We may have a tendency to blame ourselves and others for things that are out of our control, feel overwhelmed by challenges, and have low self-esteem.

Being in a negative mindset can have many negative effects on our health and well-being, including premature aging. Research has shown that chronic stress, anxiety, and depression can lead to the production of cortisol, a stress hormone that can accelerate the aging process.

It can also lead to inflammation and oxidative stress, which can damage our cells and contribute to age-related diseases.
Moreover, being in a negative mindset can lead to unhealthy habits such as poor diet, binge eating junk foods, lack of exercise, feelings of low self worth, feelings that nobody cares and inadequate sleep, which can also accelerate the aging process.

Fortunately, there are many ways to shift out of a negative mindset and promote a more positive outlook on life. Some strategies include practicing mindfulness, gratitude, and self-compassion, seeking support from loved ones, engaging in positive self-talk, and focusing on self-care.

MINDSET - POSITIVE

Being in a positive mindset means having a positive and optimistic attitude towards life. It's characterised by positive thoughts, feelings, and beliefs that can lead to a sense of happiness, well-being, and fulfilment.

When we're in a positive mindset, we tend to focus on the positive aspects of our lives and feel more grateful and content. We may have a tendency to take care of ourselves better, have more confidence in our abilities, and be more resilient in the face of challenges.

Being in a positive mindset can have many positive effects on our health and well-being, including keeping us youthful-looking. Research has shown that positive emotions can lead to the production of oxytocin, a hormone that can reduce stress, lower inflammation, and improve our immune function.

This can help slow down the aging process and keep us looking and feeling younger.
Moreover, being in a positive mindset can lead to healthy habits such as regular exercise, healthy eating, and good sleep habits, which can also help us maintain a youthful appearance.

Some ways to cultivate a positive mindset include practicing gratitude, engaging in positive self-talk, focusing on the present moment, and finding joy in everyday activities.

MINDSET - EMPOWERED

Feeling empowered is a sense of confidence and control over one's life and choices. It's the feeling of having the tools, resources, and knowledge necessary to make informed decisions and take positive actions. Feeling empowered is essential for personal growth, self-esteem, and achieving one's goals.

When you feel empowered, you have a sense of agency and autonomy in your life. You feel capable of handling challenges and making positive changes, and you trust in your own abilities and decisions. Empowerment can come from various sources, including learning new skills, gaining knowledge, and expanding your worldview.

Having positive, supportive relationships with family, friends, or mentors can help you feel empowered and encourage you to take risks and pursue your goals. Achieving personal goals, whether small or significant, can boost your self-confidence and make you feel empowered.

Standing up for yourself or others and making a positive impact in your community can help you feel empowered and make a difference.
Feeling empowered can lead to various benefits, including improved self-esteem, better decision-making, and a greater sense of fulfilment and purpose in life. It can also help you overcome obstacles and challenges with resilience and confidence.

MINDSET - DISEMPOWERED BY A PARTNER

Being disempowered in a relationship means feeling powerless, helpless, or without control. It can happen when one partner consistently dominates the relationship, making all the decisions and controlling the other partner's behaviour. It can also occur when one partner consistently dismisses the other partner's thoughts, feelings, and needs, leaving the other partner feeling ignored and unimportant.

Some signs that you may be disempowered in a relationship include feeling like you don't have a voice: If you feel like your opinions, thoughts, and feelings are constantly dismissed or ignored, you may feel like you don't have a voice in the relationship. You may feel like you're not being heard or that your perspective doesn't matter.

Feeling like you're walking on eggshells: If you're constantly worried about upsetting your partner or causing conflict, you may be disempowered in the relationship. You may feel like you have to be careful about what you say or do, in order to avoid your partner's anger or disapproval.

If you feel like you're always giving in to your partner's demands or needs, you may be disempowered in the relationship. You may feel like you're sacrificing your own needs and desires in order to keep the peace. This can also lead to feeling like you're not respected: If you feel like your partner doesn't respect you or your boundaries, you may be disempowered. You may feel like your partner doesn't take your concerns seriously or doesn't value your opinions.

Being disempowered in a relationship can be damaging to your self-esteem, your mental health, and your overall well-being. If you recognise these signs in your relationship, it's important to take steps to address them. This may involve having an honest conversation with your partner, seeking counselling or therapy, or even ending the relationship if necessary.

I had a partnership and marriage for 30 years and the last ten years I became increasing disempowered. Our communication was very one sided and our relationship was not good for my emotional health. It got to the stage where it seemed that my presence in his life was the trigger for him feeling angry and upset and full of blame for where we had come to in our lives.

Even though we had a lot of love for each other, it just wasn't enough anymore and I ended the marriage to the man I believed was my soul mate for our mental and emotional health. Life is too short to just keep at a relationship if it has broken down on many levels, disrupting the aging process can also mean making the big decisions to change your life path with the person you are with.

MINDSET - WALLOWING

"Wallowing" is a term that can be used to describe someone who is deeply immersed in negative emotions or experiences and seems to be stuck in a cycle of negativity. When someone is wallowing, they may be dwelling on past mistakes, feeling sorry for themselves, or focusing on their problems without actively seeking solutions.

For example, if someone experiences a difficult breakup and spends all their time moping around, replaying memories of the relationship, and refusing to engage in any activities or socialising, they might be said to be wallowing in their sorrow.

Wallowing can be a natural response to difficult or traumatic events, but it can also become a pattern of behaviour that prevents someone from moving forward and finding solutions. In some cases, wallowing can even lead to depression or other mental health issues.

If someone you know is wallowing, it's important to offer support and encouragement while also gently encouraging them to seek help if necessary. Encouraging them to take small steps towards improving their situation can also be helpful, such as suggesting they take a walk outside or try a new activity.

MINDSET - JOY

Being joyous is a state of being characterised by happiness, delight and contentment. It is a feeling of inner peace and fulfilment that comes from living in the present moment and finding joy in the simple things in life. When we are in a joy state, we are more likely to experience positive emotions such as love, gratitude, and awe. The key components of joy are mindfulness and gratitude.

Embracing joy leads to numerous benefits, including reduced stress, improved mood, increased resilience, enhanced immune system, lower blood pressure, and better sleep quality.
We may also be more creative, productive, and resilient in the face of challenges. There are many benefits to being joyous. Psychologically, it can reduce stress and anxiety, improve mood and overall well-being, and increase resilience in the face of adversity.

Physically, it can boost the immune system, lower blood pressure, and promote better sleep.
One of the keys to being joyous is practicing gratitude. Gratitude involves focusing on the positive aspects of life and appreciating the simple things that bring us joy, such as spending time with loved ones, enjoying a beautiful sunset, or savouring a delicious, healthy meal.

For instance, consider the story of Anna, who started writing a thank-you note to a friend each week, expressing her appreciation for their support and kindness. This practice not only helped her strengthen her friendships but also fostered a greater sense of gratitude and joy in her life.

Another important aspect of being joyous is mindfulness. Mindfulness involves being fully present in each moment and experiencing it with curiosity and openness, which can help you appreciate life's beauty and find joy in small things.

While it may seem difficult to cultivate joy in today's fast-paced and often stressful world, there are many practices that can help. These may include meditation, spending time in nature, practicing acts of kindness, and engaging in activities that bring us pleasure and fulfilment.
Dancing around your lounge room singing your favourite tunes will always immediately get you into a joy state and whilst there, it's easy to expand on your feelings of joy and gratitude.

MINDSET - HOW TO SHIFT YOUR PERSPECTIVE

Our mindset plays a crucial role in our overall well-being, and having a positive outlook can help us to overcome challenges, cope with stress, and find joy in our daily lives. However, it's not always easy to maintain a positive mindset, especially when faced with difficult situations or negative emotions. Here are some tips on how to shift your perspective from negative to positive:

1. Practice Gratitude
Gratitude is a powerful tool for cultivating a positive mindset. Take time each day to reflect on the things you're grateful for, whether it's your health, your relationships, or simply the beauty of the natural world. Focusing on the good things in your life can help to shift your perspective from negativity to positivity.

2. Challenge Negative Thoughts
Negative thoughts can be like a runaway train, quickly spiralling out of control. Challenge negative thoughts by asking yourself if they're really true, and if there's another way to view the situation. Try to reframe negative thoughts into more positive ones, focusing on solutions rather than problems.

3.   Practice Self-Care

Taking care of yourself is essential for maintaining a positive mindset. Make time for activities that bring you joy and relaxation, whether it's reading a book, taking a bath, or going for a walk. Additionally, prioritise getting enough sleep, eating a healthy diet, and exercising regularly to support your physical and mental health.

4.   Surround Yourself with Positive People

The people we surround ourselves with can have a significant impact on our mindset. Seek out positive, supportive people who uplift and encourage you, and try to minimise time spent with those who bring you down.

5.   Focus on Solutions

When faced with a challenge, try to focus on solutions rather than problems. Rather than getting bogged down by what's not working, brainstorm ways to overcome the obstacle and move forward. This can help to shift your perspective from negativity to positivity, and empower you to take action to improve your situation.

It Has to Matter to Your Mind, What Goes in Your Mouth

DIET - INTERMITTANT FASTING

This is my favourite way to eat and the only way I have found that keeps my weight stable as I age. Intermittent fasting has become a popular trend in recent years, and for good reason. Not only can it help you lose weight, but it may also help reduce the signs of aging and improve overall health and well-being.

To disrupt your aging process, it is important to be a weight that is not too heavy for your skeletal frame as you age, because the body doesn't need the added strain that carrying excess fat, places on our joints and our heart.

Many of us have tried lots of fad diets over the years, only to find that the weight comes back on and sometimes more than we initially lost.
That then leads to us feeling that diets don't work and a lot of the time they don't. Intermittent fasting isn't a diet, it is a way of eating that challenges the way we have been brought up, with eating at set times and eating three meals a day.

Intermittent fasting involves cycling between periods of eating and periods of fasting, typically with a daily eating window of 8-10 hours and a fasting window of 14-16 hours. During the fasting window, you consume no calories, only water or other non-caloric beverages. We really don't need to eat as much food when we are older as we did when we were younger as we don't need the addd fuel with a metabolism that is aging.

One of the key benefits of intermittent fasting for weight loss is that it can help reduce your overall caloric intake, which can lead to weight loss over time. It may also help boost metabolism and improve insulin sensitivity, which can further aid in weight loss.

In addition to weight loss, intermittent fasting has also been shown to have age disrupting benefits. Studies suggest that intermittent fasting can help improve cellular repair mechanisms, reduce oxidative stress, and improve overall cellular function. This can lead to a reduction in the signs of aging, such as wrinkles, age spots, and other skin imperfections.

This has certainly happened to me, I find my skin is glowing, I have less wrinkles on my face and body and no tired looking grooves on my face. I have been following this way of eating for years and its the best I've ever tried and the easiest to stick to.

Intermittent fasting has also been linked to improved brain function, increased energy levels, and a reduced risk of chronic diseases such as heart disease, diabetes, and cancer.

DIET - CARBS

Carbohydrates, such as those found in white bread, pasta, and rice, are an important source of energy for the body. However, consuming too many carbs, especially at dinner and before bed, can lead to weight gain and other health issues.

When we eat carbs, our bodies break them down into glucose, which is then used for energy or stored as glycogen in the liver and muscles. However, if we consume more carbs than we need for energy, the excess glucose is stored as fat, leading to weight gain over time.

Eating carbs at night can be particularly problematic, as our bodies are less active while we sleep, meaning we're less likely to burn off any excess glucose. This can lead to a spike in blood sugar levels and an increase in insulin production, which can lead to weight gain and other health problems.

To avoid these issues, it's best to limit your carb intake, especially at dinner and before bed. Instead, opt for protein and healthy fats, which are less likely to be stored as fat and can help keep you feeling full and satisfied.

Some good options for dinner and before bed might include lean proteins like chicken or fish, vegetables, and healthy fats like avocado or nuts. By making these small changes to your diet, you can help avoid weight gain and other health issues associated with excessive carb intake, while still enjoying a balanced and healthy diet.

DIET - DAIRY

Switching from full-fat milk and yogurt to no-fat options can offer a range of health benefits, including weight management and improved heart health. Full-fat dairy products are high in calories and saturated fats, which can lead to weight gain and an increased risk of heart disease. By switching to no-fat or low-fat options, you can significantly reduce your calorie and fat intake, making it easier to maintain a healthy weight.

In addition to weight management, no-fat dairy products can also be beneficial for heart health. Research has shown that consuming high amounts of saturated fats, which are found in full-fat dairy products, can lead to an increased risk of heart disease.

By switching to no-fat or low-fat options, you can reduce your saturated fat intake and help protect your heart.

It's important to note that while no-fat dairy products may offer some health benefits, they may also contain added sugars or other ingredients to improve flavour and texture. Be sure to read the labels carefully and opt for products with minimal added sugars and other additives.

DIET - DITCH THE MAYO

Mayonnaise is a popular condiment that is often used to add flavour and creaminess to sandwiches, salads, and other dishes. However, despite its popularity, mayonnaise is not considered a healthy choice due to its high calorie and fat content.

Mayonnaise is typically made with oil, egg yolks, and vinegar or lemon juice, all of which can be high in calories and saturated fats. In fact, just one tablespoon of mayonnaise can contain around 100 calories and 10 grams of fat, much of which is unhealthy saturated fat.

Consuming high amounts of saturated fats can lead to a range of health issues, including weight gain, high cholesterol levels, and an increased risk of heart disease. In addition, mayonnaise can also be high in sodium and other additives, which can further contribute to health problems over time.

While some brands of mayonnaise may offer no-fat or low-fat options, these may still contain added sugars or other ingredients to improve flavour and texture. As such, it's generally recommended to limit your consumption of mayonnaise and opt for healthier condiments like mustard, hummus, avocado or lemon juice.

DIET - COCONUT OIL

Coconut oil is a popular cooking oil that is often touted for its potential health benefits. Unlike many other cooking oils, coconut oil is high in medium-chain triglycerides (MCTs), which are a type of fat that is quickly metabolised by the body and can provide a range of health benefits.

One of the key benefits of cooking with coconut oil is that it is more stable at high temperatures than other oils, making it a better choice for cooking methods like frying or roasting. This is because coconut oil has a high smoke point, which means that it can be heated to high temperatures without breaking down and releasing harmful compounds.

In addition to its stability at high temperatures, coconut oil may also offer a range of other health benefits. Studies have shown that MCTs, which are abundant in coconut oil, can help boost metabolism, improve cognitive function, and even aid in weight loss.

Coconut oil is also popular to use as a body moisturiser and deep conditioner on your hair, so it has a multitude of uses. MCT oil has very little smell, so when used on your body, it won't clash with your favourite fragrance and it is absorbed into the skin beautifully without leaving an oily surface residue.

DIET - SUGAR

Sugar is a common ingredient in many processed foods and beverages, but it's also a major contributor to a range of health problems, including obesity, diabetes, and heart disease. As such, many people are looking for healthier alternatives to sugar, and one popular option is stevia.

Stevia is a natural sweetener that is derived from the leaves of the stevia plant. Unlike sugar, stevia contains zero calories and has no effect on blood sugar levels, making it a healthier choice for people looking to reduce their sugar intake.

In addition to being calorie-free and low-glycemic, stevia has also been shown to offer a range of other health benefits. Studies have found that stevia may help improve insulin sensitivity, lower blood pressure, and even reduce the risk of certain types of cancer.

One of the key benefits of stevia is that it can be used in place of sugar in a variety of recipes and beverages, making it an easy and convenient switch for people looking to reduce their sugar intake. Stevia is also available in a range of forms, including liquid drops and powder, making it a versatile choice for all your sweetening needs.

As we age, it's common for some of us to experience aches and pains in our joints. While there are many factors that can contribute to joint pain, research suggests that consuming too much sugar may be one of them. From personal experience, I know this to be true with my body.

Sugar consumption can have a range of negative effects on the body beyond just arthritis. Excessive sugar intake can lead to weight gain, which can increase the risk of developing other health problems such as diabetes, heart disease, and stroke.

It can also contribute to inflammation throughout the body, which can worsen conditions such as asthma, allergies, and skin conditions like acne. Sugar consumption has also been linked to an increased risk of certain types of cancer, including breast, colon, and pancreatic cancer.

If you are part of the population that also has tinnitus, a constant ringing in your head, sugar will always raise the noise volume. In addition, consuming too much sugar can lead to dental problems such as cavities and tooth decay. It's important to be mindful of your sugar intake and strive to consume it in moderation to maintain overall health and wellness.

DIET - PORTION SIZE

When it comes to maintaining a healthy diet and keeping your body weight stable, portion size and protein intake are both key factors to consider. Eating the right portion sizes can help us maintain a healthy weight, while ensuring we get enough protein is important for maintaining muscle mass, supporting healthy bones, and promoting overall wellness.

So, what exactly is a healthy portion size? While it can vary depending on factors like age, gender, and activity level, a general guideline is to aim for a serving of protein about the size of your palm, and to fill the rest of your plate with a variety of colourful fruits and vegetables, whole grains, and healthy fats.

It's also important to be mindful of portion sizes when it comes to snacks and desserts, as overindulging in these can quickly add up and lead to weight gain.

My advice is to not buy snacks when you shop and don't have them in the house. If you are really craving something, my rule of thumb is that I have to commit and get in the car and drive to go and get it. Snacks and junk food are too easy to consume if we reach into the cupboard and they are already there.

In addition to portion sizes, getting enough protein is also important for an aging body. As we age, our bodies become less efficient at building and maintaining muscle mass, which can lead to a range of issues like weakness, falls, and reduced mobility. By incorporating protein-rich foods like lean meats, fish, eggs, beans, and nuts into our diets, we can help support healthy muscle mass, bones, and overall wellness.

DIET - TIMING

Eating meals late at night and then going to sleep can have negative effects on our bodies, as our digestive systems and sleep cycles are closely linked. When we eat a large meal, our bodies need time to digest the food and absorb the nutrients, which can take several hours. Going to sleep soon after eating can disrupt this process and lead to a range of issues.

One of the main concerns with eating late and then sleeping is that it can lead to weight gain. When we eat late at night, our bodies are more likely to store the calories as fat, as we don't have time to burn them off before we go to sleep. Additionally, eating late can disrupt our natural hunger and fullness cues, making it harder to manage our food intake and leading to overeating.

Eating late at night can also disrupt our sleep cycles, leading to issues like insomnia, disrupted sleep, and fatigue. When we go to bed with a full stomach, our bodies have to work harder to digest the food, which can lead to discomfort and indigestion. This can make it harder to fall asleep and stay asleep, leading to a range of issues like daytime fatigue and decreased productivity.

Instead, try to eat your main meal at lunch time or mid afternoon and have a protein drink for dinner. This can help support healthy digestion, reduce the risk of weight gain, and promote better sleep and overall wellness.

DIET - RAW FOOD

Raw food diets have become increasingly popular in recent years, with many people claiming that they offer a range of health benefits. The basic idea behind a raw food diet is to eat foods that haven't been cooked or processed, which proponents claim can help preserve the natural vitamins, minerals, and enzymes in food.

One of the main benefits of eating raw food is that it can help support healthy digestion. Raw foods are typically high in fibre, which can help promote regular bowel movements and prevent constipation. Additionally, raw foods are often easier for the body to digest, as they contain natural enzymes that help break down food and improve nutrient absorption.

Another benefit of eating raw food is that it can help support healthy weight management. Raw foods are typically low in calories and high in nutrients, which can help keep you feeling full and satisfied without overeating. Additionally, eating a raw food diet can help reduce the amount of processed and high-calorie foods in your diet, which can contribute to weight gain and other health issues.

Eating raw food can also help promote healthy skin, hair, and nails. Raw foods are often high in antioxidants, which can help protect against free radical damage and oxidative stress. This can help reduce the signs of aging and improve the overall appearance of your skin, hair, and nails.
I'm a big fan of a big bowl of salad and some protein to go with it. Fish, chicken, red meat, whatever you like but no pasta or rice or starchy stuff.

DIET - BONE BROTH

Bone broth is the clear, protein rich liquid obtained by simmering meaty joints and bones in water. It distinguishes itself from stock due to its lengthy cooking time. Much like stock it can be used as a base for soups, stews and risottos.

Bone broth is a rich, nutritious food that contains protein, collagen, and minerals like iron, calcium, magnesium and phosphorus. It may hep improve bone and joint health, promote weight loss and improve your hair, skin and nails. It's also great for gut health.
Collagen from bone broth is critical if you want to optimise your overall health. I have tried other forms of collagen that came in powdered form but nothing beats the improvement I have witnessed in my skin and my overall health as bone broth.

I include a cup of bone broth in my daily diet as it contains the purest form of collagen to support your muscles, bones and joints, as well as your hair skin and nails. I use an Australian brand called Saname that comes in powder form. There are many delicious flavours of bone broths and collagen broths and you can order yours here.

DIET - JUNK FOOD

When it comes to maintaining a healthy diet, one of the best things you can do is to avoid buying junk food when you shop for groceries. Junk food, such as candy, chips, and soft drinks, are often high in calories, sugar, and unhealthy fats, and provide little to no nutritional value. We all know it is bad for us and makes us fat and unhealthy.

The more we eat, the more we want because it triggers the brains reward centre and creates a cycle of cravings and overeating. So when you shop, don't buy any chips or biscuits or chocolate or cereals that are full of sugar and bad fats and that you know are unhealthy.

If its not in the cupboard to easily satisfy your craving, its much harder to eat it. If I'm craving chocolate, which is my weakness, I have to really commit to my craving and get in the car, drive to the shops and get it. Don't make it easy for yourself.

Master your mind and your cravings. Opt for fruit or a big glass of water or my favourite and best thing I do is have a glass of chocolate flavoured collagen drink from Saname, it completely satisfies my cravings, gives me a feeling of fullness and fills my body with nutrients. It's a total win/win.

Or do something physical like some of your exercises and some bench presses at the kitchen counter to retrain your brain and distract your craving onto more healthy things.

DIET - SAY NO TO BATTERED FOOD

Batter is a mixture of flour, eggs, and milk or water that is used to coat food before it is fried or baked. While batter can make food taste crispy and delicious, it is not a healthy choice for several reasons. You already know this I'm sure, so here is a gentle reminder why batter is not a good choice.

1. High in calories: Batter is usually made from flour, which is a carbohydrate that is high in calories. When the flour is mixed with eggs and milk or water to make batter, the calorie count increases, making it an unhealthy choice for people who are trying to maintain a healthy weight.

2. High in fat: When food is coated in batter and fried, it absorbs a lot of oil or fat, which can make it high in calories and unhealthy for the heart. This is especially true for deep-fried foods, such as onion rings and fried chicken.

3. Low in nutrients: Batter is low in nutrients and is not a good source of vitamins or minerals. Instead of providing essential nutrients, batter can contribute to weight gain and unhealthy eating habits.

4. Linked to health problems: Eating too much fried food that is coated in batter has been linked to health problems such as obesity, high blood pressure, and heart disease.

Move it or Lose it

MANY WOMEN GAIN WEIGHT DURING THIS MENOPAUSAL TRANSITION AND THE BLAME FOR THIS IS OFTEN PLACED ON TREATMENTS FOR MENOPAUSE, INCLUDING HORMONE THERAPY. HOWEVER, THERE IS NO SCIENTIFIC PROOF THAT THAT'S TRUE.

Age and lifestyle choices are the main culprits, because as we age our metabolism slows down, our lean body mass decreases, whilst body fat accumulates during adulthood. Women can become less physically active in their 40's, 50's and 60's burning fewer calories by being less active, which increases weight and fat mass. Energy in and energy out. If you take in too much fuel and don't burn it off, then you will literally wear it. The old saying from my grandmother's day was a minute on the lips = an inch on the hips.

Several studies have shown that perimenopause, regardless of age, is associated with increased fat in the abdomen as well as decreased lean body mass, where the pear shaped woman transitions to a more apple shaped body. Regardless of how it happens and the obvious health issues, the effect of excess weight during this time really puts pressure on tendons and joints, which can add to your feelings.

You are at a stage where things are changing with your body. Your joints can start to hurt and become weak. You may be experiencing pain in your hips or knees, hands or fingers. Your oestrogen level drops dramatically during the perimenopause/menopause and then remains low afterwards. But if your oestrogen levels are low, your tendons will take longer to recover from a bout of exercise than when your hormone levels were normal, because your body is not as effective in producing new collagen fibres.

Ligaments are often stressed because of failing muscles and surrounding tendons causing them to work harder than what they're intended to. Your ankles, and other ligament-prominent areas, (knee, shoulder, hand/wrist, foot, and pelvis), are also a key reflection of your health, especially hormonal health, as hormonal levels and fluctuations directly affect ligament receptors and tissue repair.

There is a well-researched connection between the hormone estrogen and ligament injuries, specifically knee ACL injuries in women, more than other ligament injuries elsewhere in the body. Joints that are under a mechanical load in the presence of estrogen are known to incur a higher rate of ligament injury due to how the hormone affects collagen synthesis – specifically the formation of fibroblasts, which are cells that make up collagen. (Collagen is the main component of connective tissue and ligaments are one of many types of connective tissue.)

Sex hormones such as estrogen and progesterone also affect water retention, and this can increase swelling within the synovium, which is the soft tissue found between joints. Hey – ligaments connect joints! So you can see how these joints can quickly become more injury prone due to pressure changes and alterations in tissue repair as a direct result of hormonal issues.

Watch your weight, your joints won't be happy with you if you are too heavy. Too much excess weight will put pressure on fragile joints, tendons and ligaments causing knee and ankle joint pain, hip pain and your hands and fingers can also be affected. Now is also not the time to throw yourself into a full on gym programme, take it easy and work your way into regular exercising.

BODY ACTIVATION FOR STRENGTH AND FITNESS

It is so important to have a fit and strong body as we age. Imagine if you were older and you slipped over at home one day and you didn't have the upper body strength to pick yourself up. That would be tragic. This happens to many older women and men.

As we age, maintaining a fit and strong body becomes increasingly important. Not only does it help us maintain our independence and quality of life, but it can also prevent a range of health issues and improve our overall well-being.
A fit and strong body allows us to maintain our independence and perform everyday activities, such as walking, climbing stairs, and carrying groceries, with ease. This can help us maintain our quality of life and avoid the need for assistance or care.

Regular exercise and strength training can help prevent a range of health issues, including heart disease, diabetes, osteoporosis, and arthritis. It can also improve our immune system, which is especially important as we age and become more susceptible to illness.

Exercise and physical activity have been shown to improve our mental health, reducing stress, anxiety, and depression. This can help us maintain a positive outlook and cope with the challenges that come with aging.

Regular exercise and strength training can increase our mobility and flexibility, reducing the risk of falls and injuries. It can also improve our balance and coordination, which is especially important as we age and become more prone to falls. A fit and strong body can improve our overall well-being, providing us with more energy, better sleep, and a greater sense of self-confidence. It can also help us stay engaged in social activities and maintain our relationships with others.

Overall, having a fit and strong body is essential for maintaining our independence, preventing health issues, improving our mental health, and enhancing our overall well-being as we age. By incorporating regular exercise and strength training into our daily routine, we can enjoy the benefits of a healthy and active lifestyle.

ACTIVATE YOUR NON- DOMINANT SIDE AND INCREASE YOUR BRAIN CAPACITY

You can actually activate your brain to use the non dominant side of your body and increase your intelligence and your brain capacity by 9%. How good is that! I actually trained myself to be ambidextrous years ago when I had a shoulder stabilisation operation at 29 from being a competitive swimmer and then a couple of years after that, I was thrown from a horse and broke my left thumb and a finger.

I actively had to spend a year making my shoulder work again, so I kept going with it and kept training my left hand and arm and I made them strong again and then just started challenging myself, to start using my left hand instead of my right. Just incase anything happened to my right, my reasoning was that I would have a reliable backup.

I became very accurate with my left hand and arm and can interchange them for more detailed work as well. So my challenge to you is, instead of doing crossword puzzles as you age to keep your brain active, Why don't you start using the other side of your brain, for your age disruption journey?

When you walk upstairs for instance, you will automatically start with the same foot each time, so try to swap feet and lead with your other foot, it will feel a bit different.

When you reach for the kettle, pick it up and pour with your other hand, train yourself to be stronger and more accurate with your other hand.

Try using your non dominant hand for all sorts of things. You will be much more aware of how you use your body and how you move and you will increase the small muscles and the large muscles in your hands, arms and shoulders by doing so.

My favourite way to really work my entire left hand side is with the children's game of totem tennis. The ball on a stick that you put in the ground. It comes with two paddles. So I use them both at the same time and compete against myself.

This is a very effective way to build the other side of your body including your legs and is great fun at the same time.

Try swapping hands for writing and other delicate tasks. Train your brain and challenge yourself, you will be very grateful that you did.

EXERCISE - EARTHING

Earthing or barefoot healing, also known as grounding, refers to the practice of walking barefoot on natural surfaces such as grass, sand, or soil. It is based on the belief that direct contact with the earth's surface can have numerous health benefits.

I do this on a daily basis, have done for years and love the connection I have to Mother Earth. I feel it quite literally grounds me and I enjoy doing my daily walking meditations and manifestations whilst I'm barefoot healing.

This practice is based on the belief that direct contact with the earth's surface can have numerous health benefits.

Here are some of the potential health benefits of earthing or barefoot healing:

1. Reduced inflammation: Earthing is believed to help reduce inflammation in the body by neutralising free radicals and reducing the production of pro-inflammatory cytokines.
2. Improved sleep: Some studies have found that earthing can improve the quality of sleep by reducing cortisol levels and promoting a more relaxed state.
3. Reduced stress and anxiety: Earthing is believed to help regulate the body's stress response by promoting a state of relaxation and reducing cortisol levels.
4. Improved circulation: Walking barefoot on natural surfaces can help stimulate the nerve endings in the soles of the feet, which can improve circulation and blood flow.
5. Pain relief: Earthing is believed to help alleviate chronic pain by reducing inflammation and improving circulation.
6. Improved immune function: Some studies have found that earthing can boost the immune system by increasing the activity of natural killer cells and reducing the production of stress hormones.
7. Improved mood: Earthing is believed to have a calming effect on the nervous system, which can help improve mood and reduce symptoms of depression and anxiety.

EXERCISE - AQUA AEROBICS

Aqua aerobics is a fun and effective way to exercise that's easy on your joints and great for people of all ages and fitness levels. It's a low-impact workout that takes place in the water, making it a great choice for anyone looking for a gentle yet effective way to get in shape.

During an aqua aerobics class, you'll perform a range of exercises that are specifically designed to be performed in the water, from jogging and jumping jacks to squats and lunges. The water provides resistance that helps to tone your muscles and increase your overall fitness level, while also reducing the impact on your joints.

Aqua aerobics is a great way to improve your cardiovascular health, build strength and endurance, and burn calories. It's also a great way to stay cool and comfortable during hot summer months, making it a popular choice for people of all ages.

To get started with aqua aerobics, all you need is a swimsuit and a willingness to try something new. Classes are often held at local pools or gyms, and are led by certified instructors who can guide you through the exercises and help you get the most out of your workout.

EXERCISE - SWIMMING

Swimming is a highly effective exercise that can help you improve your cardiovascular health, build strength and endurance, and reduce stress. It's a low-impact workout that's easy on your joints, making it a great choice for people of all ages and fitness levels.

When you swim, your entire body is engaged in a full-body workout that helps to tone your muscles and increase your overall fitness level. It's also a great way to improve your flexibility and coordination, as well as reduce your risk of chronic health conditions such as diabetes and heart disease.

Swimming can be enjoyed in a variety of settings, from public pools to natural bodies of water. Whether you're doing laps or just splashing around, swimming is a great way to stay cool and comfortable during hot summer months while also getting in a great workout.

To get started with swimming, all you need is access to a pool and a willingness to get wet. Whether you're a beginner or an experienced swimmer, there are a variety of different strokes and techniques you can use to improve your fitness.

If you're looking for a highly effective exercise that's gentle on your joints and can help you improve your overall fitness level, you can also workout with a pool noodle or water weights and a kick board. Do stretching exercises pushing against the weight of the water, which improves leg, arm and shoulder fitness whilst enjoying the benefits of being in the water.

EXERCISE - HAND WEIGHTS

Using hand weights is a great way to add resistance to your workout and increase the intensity of your exercises. It's a simple yet highly effective way to build strength and tone your muscles, and it's easy to incorporate into your existing workout routine.

Hand weights, also known as dumbbells, come in a variety of sizes and weights, making it easy to find the perfect fit for your fitness level and goals. You can use hand weights to perform a range of exercises, from bicep curls and tricep extensions to shoulder presses and lunges.

Using hand weights can help you improve your overall fitness level, increase your strength and endurance, and boost your metabolism. It can also help you build lean muscle mass, which can help you burn more calories even when you're at rest.

To get started with using hand weights, all you need is a set of dumbbells. Start with a weight that feels comfortable for you, and gradually increase the weight as you feel more comfortable and your strength improves.

If you don't have weights reach for cans of food to start with from the cupboard. Its always good to start with a light weight first. You can also use full water bottles.

EXERCISE - SEATED

If you're not as fit and agile as you would like to be and have not done regular exercise for a while you can do seated exercises. There are plenty of gentle exercises you can do to get started. Whether you're recovering from an injury, have limited mobility, or simply want to incorporate more movement into your day, these exercises can help.

1. Seated Leg Raises: Sit upright in your chair with your feet flat on the ground. Slowly lift one leg off the floor and extend it out in front of you, holding for a few seconds. Lower your leg back down and repeat with the other leg. This exercise strengthens your leg muscles and improves circulation.
2. Seated Knee Lifts: Sit upright in your chair with your feet flat on the ground. Lift one knee towards your chest, holding it there for a few seconds before lowering it back down. Repeat with the other knee. This exercise helps to strengthen your core and leg muscles.
3. Seated Marching: Sit upright in your chair with your feet flat on the ground. Lift one foot off the ground and lower it back down, then repeat with the other foot. This exercise improves your balance and strengthens your leg muscles.
4. Seated Arm Raises: Sit upright in your chair with your arms at your sides. Slowly raise both arms out to the side, keeping them straight, and hold them there for a few seconds. Lower your arms back down and repeat. This exercise helps to strengthen your upper body.
5. Seated Shoulder Rolls: Sit upright in your chair with your arms at your sides. Slowly roll your shoulders forward in a circular motion, then reverse the motion and roll them backwards. This exercise helps to improve your posture and relieve tension in your shoulders.

EXERCISE - MUSCLE ACTIVATION - TUMMY

When I was a young woman the saying was.. stomach in shoulders back chest out! Most of us have been told at some point in our lives to "suck in our stomachs" or "hold our stomachs in." While it may seem like a superficial habit meant to make us look slimmer, there are actually important health benefits to activating our stomach muscles in this way.

When we hold our stomach in, we engage our core muscles, including the rectus abdominis, transverse abdominis, and obliques. It also supports our lower back. Here are some potential benefits of activating these muscles:

1. Improved Posture

Activating our core muscles can help improve our posture by providing support for our spine and pelvis. This can help reduce the risk of back pain and improve our overall alignment.

2. Stronger Core

Holding our stomach in can also help strengthen our core muscles over time. By engaging these muscles regularly, we can improve their tone and endurance, which can help with activities like lifting, twisting, and bending.

3. Better Breathing

Engaging our core muscles can also improve our breathing by allowing us to take deeper, more efficient breaths. This is because the diaphragm, a muscle involved in breathing, is connected to the core muscles and can be better supported when they are activated.

4. Improved Digestion

Finally, activating our core muscles can also improve our digestion by promoting better circulation and movement in the digestive tract. This can help reduce bloating and constipation, and promote overall digestive health.

MUSCLE ACTIVATION - GLUTES - BOTTOMS

The glutes, or the muscles in your buttocks, are some of the largest and strongest muscles in your body. They play a crucial role in many of the movements we make, from walking and running to sitting and standing up. However, many of us don't use our glutes as effectively as we could, which can lead to a host of problems.

One of the biggest reasons to activate your glutes is to prevent injury. When your glutes are weak or inactive, other muscles in your body have to work harder to compensate, which can lead to strain and injury. Activating your glutes can help distribute the workload more evenly and reduce the risk of injury.

Another reason to activate your glutes is to improve your posture. When your glutes are weak, it can cause your pelvis to tilt forward, which can lead to lower back pain and other posture-related issues. By strengthening your glutes, you can help keep your pelvis in a neutral position, which can improve your overall posture and reduce pain.

Squeezing your glutes, also known as glute activation, is a simple and effective way to activate your glute muscles. By squeezing your glutes, you can help wake up these muscles and improve their strength and function.

Glute activation is especially important for those who spend a lot of time sitting, as sitting can cause your glutes to become weak and inactive. By regularly activating your glutes, you can help counteract the negative effects of sitting and improve your overall physical health.

To activate your glutes by squeezing them, start by standing with your feet hip-width apart. Then, squeeze your glutes together as tightly as you can, holding the contraction for a few seconds before releasing. You can also try squeezing one glute at a time, or squeezing both glutes while lying on your back with your knees bent.

You can also activate your vaginal muscles at the same time. Activating your vaginal muscles and pelvic floor is crucial to maintaining good sexual health and preventing issues like urinary incontinence. One way to do this is by performing Kegel exercises, which involve squeezing and relaxing the muscles that control urination and sexual function.

To perform a Kegel exercise, start by emptying your bladder completely. Then, contract the muscles around your vagina and anus as if you are trying to stop the flow of urine mid-stream. Hold the contraction for a few seconds, then relax the muscles and repeat.

You can also stop urination mid stream by squeezing your muscles, this also helps to activate them.

Regularly performing Kegel exercises can help improve vaginal tone, enhance sexual sensation, and reduce the risk of urinary incontinence.
So, start incorporating Kegel exercises into your daily routine and start reaping the benefits of a strong and healthy pelvic floor.

Primal Therapies

Primal therapy is a type of psychotherapy that aims to help people connect with and process repressed emotions and traumas from their childhood. It was developed by psychologist Arthur Janov in the 1960s and gained popularity in the 1970s.

The foundation of primal therapy is the belief that emotional pain from past experiences can become suppressed in the body and cause psychological and physical symptoms in the present. Through primal therapy, individuals are encouraged to express and release these emotions through intense sessions of cathartic screaming, crying, and physical movements.

By facing and processing these deep-seated emotions, individuals may experience a greater sense of self-awareness and emotional freedom, leading to improved relationships, reduced anxiety and depression, and an overall sense of well-being.

While some critics argue that primal therapy is overly confrontational and lacks scientific evidence, proponents of the therapy maintain that it can be an effective tool for healing deep emotional wounds and promoting personal growth.

I first discovered primal therapy when I was 15. Not from any reading or education I had received on the subject but from a purely primal need to release the pent up emotions I was feeling in my body.
I was raised by a mother that was a narcissist and in my home life I was not receiving the sort of love that I required from the main nurturer, instead the main emotion I was receiving was jealousy.

I was a competitive swimmer from the age of 12 and at 15 I was training with my father in the afternoons at a local club. This was as much for him to be fit and healthy as it was for me and it was here that I started releasing my frustrations and anger by screaming under the water.

When you scream in water, no-one can hear you so I was in a very safe environment. With each lap I would be pushing myself physically, whilst screaming out all my emotions, so at the end of a session I was completed exhausted and able to go home and face my mother, completely empty of any residual negativity towards her and ready to live another day.

SCREAM THERAPY

Scream therapy, also known as primal scream therapy, is a form of therapy that involves vocalising intense emotions through screams, shouts, and other vocalisations. The therapy is based on the idea that releasing pent-up emotions through primal screaming can help individuals heal from emotional and psychological distress.

The theory behind scream therapy is that emotional pain and trauma can become trapped in the body, leading to physical and psychological symptoms. By vocalising these emotions through screaming and other forms of expression, individuals can release this trapped energy and promote healing.

I have introduced scream therapy to several of my coaching clients with great results as it a short sharp way of relieving and removing pent up emotions.

While scream therapy may be beneficial for some individuals, it is not without controversy. Some critics argue that the therapy is not backed by scientific evidence and may even be harmful for some individuals, particularly those with certain mental health conditions.

Despite the controversy, some individuals report that scream therapy has helped them cope with emotional pain, reduce stress and anxiety, and improve their overall well-being. It is important to note, however, that scream therapy should not be used as a substitute for medical treatment or therapy for mental health conditions.

LAUGHTER THERAPY

Laughter therapy, also known as laughter yoga or laughter meditation, is a form of therapy that involves deliberate laughter as a form of physical and emotional release. The therapy is based on the idea that laughter has a range of physical and psychological benefits, and that intentional laughter can be used as a tool for healing and well-being.

During a laughter therapy session, individuals are encouraged to engage in various exercises and activities that promote laughter and playfulness. This may include group exercises, such as laughing in unison, fake laughter, and playful interactions with others. The therapist may also use humour and laughter-inducing techniques to help individuals let go of stress and anxiety.

The benefits of laughter therapy are thought to be both physical and psychological. Physically, laughter therapy can reduce stress hormones, boost the immune system, and improve cardiovascular health. It can also promote relaxation and relieve tension in the body.
Psychologically, laughter therapy can reduce anxiety and depression, improve mood, and increase feelings of well-being. It can also promote social connection and improve communication skills.

I have also used laughter therapy with some of my clients directly following a screaming session. To elevate their mood, help release any residual negativity that is attached to the scream therapy and instantly activate positivity and joy.

While laughter therapy may seem unconventional, it has gained popularity in recent years as a complementary therapy for a range of physical and mental health conditions. It is often used alongside traditional medical treatments and therapy to promote overall well-being and improve quality of life.

SMASHING STUFF

In recent years, a new type of therapy has emerged that involves smashing and destroying objects as a form of stress relief. This therapy, known as "rage therapy" or "anger room therapy," has gained popularity as a unique way to release pent-up emotions and relieve stress.

During a rage therapy session, participants are typically provided with protective gear, such as helmets and safety glasses, and given a selection of items to destroy, such as old electronics, dishes, or furniture. They are then encouraged to let out their frustrations by smashing, breaking, and destroying these items.

I find smashing stuff is great fun and using your physicality to bash the crap out of something is a great form of stress relief. I have introduced this to my son and his friends when he was in his teens and it provided great stress relief for them. There was also the added bonus of experiencing the perceived naughtiness behind breaking a piece of furniture which added to the therapy of the situation.

Here are some potential benefits of rage therapy:

1.   Stress Relief

Rage therapy can be an effective way to release pent-up stress and tension. Breaking and smashing objects can provide a physical outlet for emotions that may be difficult to express verbally. It can also provide a sense of release and catharsis, leaving participants feeling more relaxed and calm.

2.   Increased Self-Awareness

Engaging in rage therapy can also provide insight into the emotions and triggers that may be causing stress and frustration in daily life. By identifying these triggers and developing coping mechanisms to manage them, participants may be better equipped to handle stress in the future.

3.   Improved Mood

Rage therapy can also be a fun and unique experience that can improve mood and increase feelings of happiness and well-being. Participants may experience a sense of empowerment and accomplishment from breaking objects and overcoming any fears or anxieties they may have had about doing so.

While rage therapy can be a fun and unique way to relieve stress, it's important to note that it's not a substitute for professional mental health treatment. If you're struggling with stress, anxiety, or other mental health issues, it's important to seek help from a licensed mental health professional.

SINGING

Singing is a universal human activity that has been enjoyed for thousands of years. Whether it's singing in the shower, belting out tunes in the car, or joining a choir, there are many reasons to sing - including some surprising health benefits. Here are some potential benefits of singing if you are unaware.

1. Improved Breathing

Singing can be a great way to improve our breathing, as it requires us to use our lungs and diaphragm in a way that promotes deep, controlled breathing. This can be especially beneficial for people with respiratory issues like asthma or COPD.

2. Reduced Stress

Singing can also be a great way to reduce stress and promote relaxation. Studies have found that singing can lower levels of the stress hormone cortisol, while increasing levels of the feel-good hormone oxytocin.

3. Boosted Immunity

Believe it or not, singing can also boost our immune system by increasing levels of immunoglobulin A, which helps fight off infections. This is because singing engages our respiratory system and promotes deeper breathing, which can help flush out toxins and improve overall health.

4. Improved Mood

Singing can also be a mood booster, as it releases endorphins - the body's natural feel-good chemicals. Singing can also be a way to express emotions and connect with others, which can help reduce feelings of loneliness and depression.

5. Increased Social Connection

Finally, singing can be a great way to connect with others and foster a sense of community. Whether it's joining a choir, singing in a group, or just sharing a favourite song with a friend, singing can be a way to bond with others and promote social connection.

Body Mechanics

BODY MECHANICS - FEET

As we get older our bodies start to age and natural wear and tear occurs, we can often feel pain and discomfort in or ankles, knees and hips and these can often be traced back to or feet being unstable. Ive been wearing orthotics since I was 28. I was competitive swimmer in high school and my stroke was breaststroke. Being a bit of a bendy person, and due to the nature of the stroke kick, the ligaments on the inside of my knees got a bit longer, so my feet rolled inward causing pain and unstable knees. Orthotics fixed this, so I'm a big fan.

Orthotics are specialised devices designed to support and correct imbalances in the feet and lower body. They are commonly used to treat a wide range of foot and lower body conditions, including plantar fasciitis, flat feet, and knee pain. Here are some of the key benefits of using orthotics:

1. Improved Foot and Lower Body Alignment: Orthotics are designed to support the feet and help align the lower body. By correcting imbalances in the feet and ankles, orthotics can help to reduce strain on the knees, hips, and lower back.

2. Reduced Pain and Discomfort: Many foot and lower body conditions can cause pain and discomfort. Orthotics are designed to provide support and cushioning to the feet, which can help to reduce pain and discomfort.

3. Enhanced Athletic Performance: Athletes often use orthotics to improve their performance and reduce the risk of injury. Orthotics can help to improve balance, stability, and shock absorption, which can lead to better performance and reduced risk of injury.

4. Customisable Fit: Orthotics can be customised to fit the specific needs of the individual. This means that your podiatrist will assess your walking style and your gait and take plaster casts of your feet so that unique shoe inserts can be tailored for you personally, leading to better results and improved comfort.

5. Reduced Risk of Future Injuries: By correcting imbalances and providing support, orthotics can help to reduce the risk of future injuries. This can be especially important for individuals who are prone to foot or lower body injuries.

MEDICAL STUFF - CHECKS YOU MUST HAVE

BOWEL CHECKS

As we age, it becomes increasingly important to monitor our bowel health. The risk of developing bowel problems, such as colon cancer, increases as we get older. By getting regular bowel checks, we can catch potential problems early and increase our chances of successful treatment.

One of the most important bowel checks for older adults is a colonoscopy. During a colonoscopy, a healthcare provider uses a flexible tube with a camera to examine the inside of the colon and rectum. This can help detect signs of cancer, polyps, or other bowel conditions.

In addition to colonoscopies, other bowel checks may include stool tests, which can help detect blood or other abnormalities in the stool, and digital rectal exams, which allow a healthcare provider to feel for abnormalities in the rectum.

It's important to note that while bowel checks can be uncomfortable or embarrassing, they are a crucial part of maintaining our health as we age. By detecting potential problems early, we can take steps to address them and prevent more serious complications down the road.
If you're unsure whether you should be getting regular bowel checks, talk to your healthcare provider. They can help determine the appropriate screening schedule based on your individual risk factors and health history.

In Australia not long after our 50th birthday we receive a free bowl check kit from the government and then again at age 55. This is a great initiative and reminder to check your poo.

BREAST CHECK

Breast cancer is one of the most common forms of cancer in women, with an estimated 1 in 8 women developing the disease at some point in their lifetime. While breast cancer can be a serious and potentially life-threatening condition, early detection is key to successful treatment and recovery. That's why it's crucial for women to have regular breast checks to monitor their breast health.

Breast checks can be performed in a variety of ways, including self-exams, clinical breast exams, and mammograms. Here are some reasons why breast checks are important:

1. Early Detection

The earlier breast cancer is detected, the more treatable it is. Breast checks can help detect abnormalities in the breast tissue, including lumps, changes in texture, or nipple discharge, that may indicate the presence of cancer. When detected early, breast cancer is often easier to treat and has a better prognosis.

2. Peace of Mind

Regular breast checks can also provide peace of mind for women who may be concerned about their breast health. By monitoring changes in the breast tissue over time, women can take a proactive approach to their health and catch any potential issues early on.

3. Risk Assessment

Breast checks can also be used to assess a woman's risk of developing breast cancer. Women who have a family history of breast cancer or other risk factors may need to have more frequent or intensive screenings to monitor their breast health.

4. Education

Breast checks can also be an opportunity for women to learn more about breast health and cancer prevention. Healthcare providers can provide information on risk factors, lifestyle changes, and preventative measures that women can take to reduce their risk of developing breast cancer.

FOR WOMEN - BREAST HEALTH

The importance of having a good fitting bra.

A good fitting bra is essential for every woman. Not only does it provide the necessary support and comfort, but it can also improve your posture, reduce discomfort, and enhance your overall appearance. Here are some reasons why having a good fitting bra is so important:

1. Provides proper support: A well-fitting bra provides the necessary support for your breasts. This can help prevent pain and discomfort, particularly during physical activity or extended periods of wear. It can also help reduce the risk of sagging and other breast-related issues.

2. Enhances your appearance: A good fitting bra can enhance your overall appearance by providing a flattering shape and lift. This can help you feel more confident and comfortable in your clothing.

3. Improves posture: A bra that fits well can help improve your posture by providing support to your chest and upper back. This can reduce strain on your neck and shoulders, and improve your overall alignment.

4. Increases comfort: A bra that fits well should feel comfortable throughout the day. It should not dig into your skin or cause irritation, and should provide the necessary support without feeling restrictive.

5. Prevents health issues: Wearing a poorly fitting bra can lead to a range of health issues, including back and neck pain, headaches, and skin irritation. A good fitting bra can help prevent these issues and ensure your overall health and well-being.

VAGINAL AND VULVA CHECKS

As women age, it becomes increasingly important to monitor the health of the vaginal and vulva areas. The risk of developing vaginal or vulvar cancer, infections, or other conditions increases as we get older. By getting regular checks and screenings, we can catch potential problems early and increase our chances of successful treatment.

One of the most important checks for women is a pelvic exam. During a pelvic exam, a healthcare provider examines the vagina, cervix, and vulva for any abnormalities, such as growths or lesions. They may also perform a Pap test, which checks for abnormal cells that could lead to cervical cancer.

It's important to note that while pelvic exams can be uncomfortable or embarrassing, they are a crucial part of maintaining women's health as they age. By detecting potential problems early, women can take steps to address them and prevent more serious complications down the road.

In addition to pelvic exams, women should also be aware of any changes or symptoms they experience in the vaginal or vulva areas, such as itching, pain, or unusual discharge. These symptoms could be a sign of an infection or other problem that requires medical attention.

If you're unsure whether you should be getting regular vaginal and vulva checks, talk to your healthcare provider. They can help determine the appropriate screening schedule based on your individual risk factors and health history.

PROSTATE CHECKS

Prostate checks are an important part of maintaining men's health as they get older. The prostate is a gland located near the bladder that plays a crucial role in male reproductive health. However, as men age, the prostate can become enlarged or develop other problems, which can lead to uncomfortable or even serious symptoms.

One of the most common prostate checks for older men is a digital rectal exam, or DRE. During a DRE, a healthcare provider inserts a lubricated, gloved finger into the rectum to feel for abnormalities in the prostate. This can help detect potential problems like prostate cancer or an enlarged prostate, which can cause urinary symptoms like difficulty urinating or frequent urination.

Another common prostate check is a prostate-specific antigen (PSA) blood test. This test measures the level of PSA, a protein produced by the prostate, in the blood. High levels of PSA can be a sign of prostate cancer or other prostate problems.

It's important to note that while prostate checks can be uncomfortable or embarrassing, they are a crucial part of maintaining men's health as they age. By detecting potential problems early, men can take steps to address them and prevent more serious complications down the road.

If you're unsure whether you should be getting regular prostate checks, talk to your healthcare provider. They can help determine the appropriate screening schedule based on your individual risk factors and health history. Don't be like your fathers and not have these checks done out of fear or embarrassment of the doctor sticking his finger up your bum. It could save your live!

Supplements

DIET -SUPPLEMENTS

These are some of the supplements I take in my everyday life on my aging disrupters journey.
The food we eat is not enough and supplements are important to support our bodies as we age.

TURMERIC AND BLACK PEPPER

Turmeric is a spice that has been used for thousands of years in traditional medicine, and modern research has shown that it has a variety of health benefits. One of the main active compounds in turmeric is called curcumin, which has anti-inflammatory and antioxidant properties.

However, the absorption of curcumin in the body can be limited, which is where black pepper comes in. Black pepper contains a compound called pipperine, which can enhance the absorption of curcumin by up to 2000%.

I have been taking this for years and I have a capsule machine and I buy both in bulk and capsule my own mix with 3 parts turmeric to one part black pepper. I find this will relieve any pain I have in my joints with in two days of taking it. I take it daily.

Here are some of the potential benefits of taking a turmeric and black pepper mix:

1. Reducing inflammation: As mentioned, curcumin has anti-inflammatory properties that can help reduce inflammation throughout the body. This may be particularly helpful for people with conditions like arthritis, which involve chronic inflammation in the joints.

2. Boosting brain function: Curcumin may also have neuroprotective properties that can help improve cognitive function and reduce the risk of neurological disorders like Alzheimer's disease.

3. Supporting heart health: Curcumin may help reduce the risk of heart disease by improving blood flow, reducing inflammation, and lowering cholesterol levels.

4. Enhancing digestion: Both turmeric and black pepper have been used to aid digestion, and the combination of the two may help relieve digestive issues like bloating, gas, and constipation.

5. Supporting weight management: Curcumin may help regulate metabolism and reduce inflammation, which could potentially aid in weight management.

MAGNESIUM

Modern living requires lots of energy. Many people make the mistake of thinking that eating more food will actually give them the energy they need, which it doesn't, so many of us turn to other stimulants such as coffee, energy drinks (full of sugar) over the counter stimulants and anything with sugar to give the quick energy boost they are craving.

We all know that we get a quick damaging burst of high energy followed by a crash, which often sends you looking for another quick fix.
This constant up and down will eventually burn out your adrenal glands. The more you force your adrenals to work in overdrive, the faster magnesium is depleted from your body. It's a vicious cycle.

Magnesium is about as close as you can get to an all-around sleep and health supplement. Magnesium is what fuels your body's internal battery and without it your cells are drain with the right energy in the right place, it is possible that everyone can thrive and flourish in today's busy society. We don't have to feel tired or overwhelmed. Because of its role as an enabler of healthy enzyme function, magnesium plays an important part in most of our physiological functions.

One of the seven essential macro minerals that the human body needs in large quantities, maintaining healthy magnesium levels protects metabolic health, stabilises mood, keeps stress in check, promotes better sleep, and contributes to heart and bone health. Magnesium supports optimum heart health, increases cellular energy production and also regulates blood sugar and glucose levels.

Magnesium deficiency is common, especially as we age and when it is low we have a higher risk of high blood pressure, poor circulation, heart attack, muscle spasms, cold hands, numbness, varicose/spider veins, panic attacks, tingling, hardening of joints and blood vessels and arthritis.
Keeping magnesium levels healthy can lead to deeper, more sound sleep.

Research indicates supplemental magnesium can improve sleep quality, have a stabilising effect on mood, as a topical spray on your body it can help to reduce the pain associated with aching joints and muscles. This whole-health mineral has been shown effective in relieving symptoms of both mild-to-moderate anxiety and mild-to-moderate depression.

Magnesium plays a critical role in maintaining bone density. Higher magnesium intake is linked to greater bone density in women. In postmenopausal women, magnesium has been shown to improve bone mass. We have all been told how important calcium is for our health and wellbeing, supporting strong bones and cartilage and joint health. While this is absolutely true, many people don't realise that calcium cannot be absorbed and put to good use in your body without magnesium.

An accumulation of non - bioavailable calcium manifests in the form of aching joints, knee and hip problems, arthritis and the deterioration of cartilage. It can also clog the arteries and cause endless physical ailments until enough magnesium is available to bring the excess calcium into balance.

Magnesium was once abundantly available in the food we eat, but is now steadily disappearing from our food supply due to modern farming techniques and large scale use of chemical fertilizer that rob the soil and the plants that grow in it of essential nutrients.

Supplementation is the only way to ensure you receive that rich supply of magnesium that your body needs everyday in order to function fully and fill you with the energy you need to live in our modern world.

Epsom salts from your pharmacy or supermarket added to your bath water for a soak will deliver the magnesium to your body as it soaks into your skin. If you don't have a bath you can soak your feet in a bucket of warm water with epsom salts. There are a few magnesium sprays on the market that are readily available from health food stores and it's handy to carry some with you if you have joint pain.

OMEGA 3 FISH OIL

Omega 3, a nutrient found in nuts, seeds, and fish, is necessary for the body as it regulates a number of functions such as skin oil production, hydration, and signs of ageing. This nutrient also benefits the conditions of depression, inflammation, and heart conditions. It helps keeps the heart, lungs, and blood vessels in good shape.

The fish oil omega 3 helps retain moisture in the skin by acting on the phospholipid bilayer, delaying ageing.

Body inflammation is one of the major causes of many skin, hair, and health conditions. Omega 3 consists of **anti-inflammatory properties** which help reduce body inflammation. They keep the skin's cell membranes in good shape, which allows cells to be hydrated.

These nutrients also help with inflammation of the digestive tract, thereby improving gut health. Taking omega 3's can also help with the skin condition psoriasis.

Omega 3 can help with osteoporosis, hot flushes vaginal dryness, depression, menstrual pain, joint pain / menopause arthritis and hypertriglyceridemia.

MELATONIN

Melatonin is a hormone that is naturally produced by the body's pineal gland. While it is well-known for its role in regulating sleep-wake cycles, recent research has shown that it also has several benefits for aging skin.

First and foremost, melatonin has antioxidant properties that help protect the skin from damage caused by free radicals. Free radicals are unstable molecules that can damage cells and contribute to aging, but melatonin helps to neutralise them and prevent their harmful effects.

Melatonin also helps to stimulate the production of collagen, which is a protein that gives skin its elasticity and firmness. As we age, the production of collagen naturally decreases, leading to wrinkles and sagging skin. By increasing collagen production, melatonin can help to reduce the appearance of fine lines and wrinkles and improve skin firmness.

Additionally, melatonin has anti-inflammatory properties that can help to reduce inflammation in the skin. Inflammation is a key factor in many skin conditions, such as acne and rosacea, and can also contribute to aging. By reducing inflammation, melatonin can help to improve overall skin health and appearance.

Overall, melatonin is a promising supplement for aging skin due to its antioxidant, collagen-boosting, and anti-inflammatory properties. It is important to note, however, that more research is needed to fully understand the benefits and potential risks of melatonin supplementation for skin health.

5HTP

5-Hydroxytryptophan commonly known as 5-HTP, is a naturally occurring amino acid that is often used as a dietary supplement to support mood and sleep. As we age, our bodies may produce less of the neurotransmitters that regulate our mood and sleep, making it more difficult to maintain optimal levels of these important chemicals.

5-HTP helps the body to produce more serotonin. Serotonin is a neurotransmitter that plays a key role in regulating mood and sleep-wake cycles. Healthy levels contribute to a positive mood and outlook and also promote restful sleep. Serotonin also plays an important role in many other of the body's functions, including digestion, appetite, and pain perception.

Because of its role in creating serotonin, 5-HTP is indirectly involved in producing melatonin, a hormone that is critical for sleep.
Because of its serotonin-boosting capability, 5-HTP may also help with other conditions, including mood problems, stress, pain, and appetite control. Low serotonin may also trigger hot flashes.

Keeping serotonin levels up may help reduce a woman's risk for hot flashes. 5-HTP has been shown in scientific studies to promote relaxation and alleviate stress and anxiety. Research also indicates 5-HTP may be effective in helping to alleviate depression.

5-HTP has also been recognised as important to appetite regulation. Higher levels of serotonin are linked to diminished appetite. Keeping serotonin levels from dipping can help keep appetite in check, and may help reduce carbohydrate cravings.

Research indicates that 5-HTP may be effective in helping people who are overweight or obese lose weight.
Scientific evidence shows 5-HTP may be able to reduce the frequency and pain of migraine headaches. Many women experience headache and migraine during menopause.

It's important to note that, as with any supplement, it's important to speak with a healthcare professional before incorporating 5-HTP into your daily routine, especially if you are taking any prescription medications or have a pre-existing medical condition. However, for aging individuals looking to support their mood, sleep, and overall health, 5-HTP may offer a natural and effective solution.

NMN

NMN, or nicotinamide mononucleotide is a compound that has gained a lot of attention in recent years for its potential anti-aging benefits. As we age, our bodies experience a decline in the production of a molecule called NAD+, which plays a crucial role in many cellular processes.
NMN has been shown to boost NAD+ levels in the body, which can have a variety of positive effects on aging.

One of the key benefits of taking NMN is its potential to improve overall energy levels. By increasing NAD+ levels, NMN can enhance the functioning of mitochondria, the cellular powerhouses that produce energy for the body. This can lead to increased physical stamina and improved exercise performance.

NMN has also been shown to have neuro-protective effects, which can help to protect against age-related cognitive decline. Studies have suggested that NMN supplementation can improve memory and learning ability in aging animals, and there is reason to believe that similar effects may be seen in humans.

Another potential benefit of NMN is its ability to improve cardiovascular health. NMN has been shown to improve blood flow and decrease inflammation, which can reduce the risk of heart disease and stroke.

Finally, NMN may also have positive effects on skin aging. As we age, our skin experiences a decline in the production of collagen, a key protein that helps to keep skin firm and elastic. NMN has been shown to increase the production of collagen in skin cells, which can lead to firmer, more youthful-looking skin.

Overall, there is a growing body of research suggesting that NMN may have a wide range of anti-aging benefits for the body. While more research is needed to fully understand its effects in humans, it is an exciting area of research that has the potential to revolutionise the way we age.

GREEN DRINKS

Green drinks that contain wheat grass, barley grass, spirulina, broccoli, kelp, parsley, and other nutrient-dense ingredients are a fantastic way to boost your overall health and wellbeing, especially as you age. These superfoods are loaded with vitamins, minerals, and antioxidants that your body needs to function at its best.

One of the main benefits of drinking green drinks is that they can help to detoxify your body. The ingredients in these drinks can help to cleanse your liver and kidneys, which are responsible for filtering out toxins and waste products from your body. This can help to improve your energy levels, reduce inflammation, and even improve the appearance of your skin.

These nutrient-dense drinks are packed with vitamins, minerals, and antioxidants that help to combat free radicals and reduce oxidative stress. This, in turn, can help to slow down the aging process, keeping your skin looking younger and more vibrant.

The high levels of vitamin C found in many green drinks can also help to boost collagen production, which is essential for maintaining healthy tendons, ligaments, and joints. Collagen is the main structural protein in our skin and connective tissues, and as we age, our bodies produce less of it. By drinking green drinks, you can give your body the nutrients it needs to maintain healthy collagen levels and keep your tendons and joints strong and supple.

Green drinks are also a great source of chlorophyll, which is a natural compound that gives plants their green colour. Chlorophyll has been shown to have a range of health benefits, including reducing inflammation, boosting immune function, and promoting healthy digestion.

In addition to chlorophyll, many green drinks also contain spirulina, which is a type of blue-green algae that is packed with protein, vitamins, and minerals. Spirulina has been shown to have powerful antioxidant and anti-inflammatory properties, which can help to protect your cells from damage and reduce your risk of chronic diseases.

Other ingredients commonly found in green drinks, such as broccoli, kelp, and parsley, are rich in vitamins and minerals that are essential for healthy aging. These ingredients can help to support your immune system, improve your digestion, and reduce your risk of age-related illnesses.
Overall, incorporating green drinks into your diet is a simple and effective way to support your overall health and wellbeing as you age. They are a great way to get more nutrients into your diet, and can help to protect your body against the effects of aging.

Skin Food - All natural stuff for your skin

SKIN CARE - ESSENTIAL OILS FOR AGING SKIN

Aging is a natural process that affects everyone, but there are many natural remedies that can help slow down the signs of aging, including essential oils. Essential oils are concentrated plant extracts that are known for their therapeutic properties, including anti-inflammatory, antioxidant, and anti-aging effects.

Some of the best essential oils in my opinion to use for aging skin include:

1. Frankincense Oil: Frankincense oil is known for its ability to promote skin cell regeneration, reduce the appearance of fine lines and wrinkles, and improve skin elasticity. It also has anti-inflammatory properties that can help soothe and calm the skin.

2. Lavender Oil: Lavender oil is known for its calming properties, but it also has anti-aging benefits. It can help reduce the appearance of fine lines and wrinkles, improve skin texture and tone, and promote skin cell regeneration.

3. Rosehip Oil: Rosehip oil is rich in antioxidants, vitamins A and C, and essential fatty acids, which make it an excellent choice for aging skin. It can help reduce the appearance of fine lines and wrinkles, improve skin texture and tone, and promote collagen production.

4. Carrot Seed Oil: Carrot seed oil is rich in antioxidants and vitamins that can help improve skin elasticity, reduce the appearance of fine lines and wrinkles, and promote skin cell regeneration. It also has anti-inflammatory properties that can help soothe and calm the skin.

5. Geranium Oil: Geranium oil is known for its ability to balance hormones and improve skin texture and tone. It can help reduce the appearance of fine lines and wrinkles, and promote skin cell regeneration.

When using essential oils on aging skin, it's important to dilute them with a carrier oil, such as jojoba oil, macadamia nut oil, almond oil or argan oil before applying them to the skin. It's also important to do a patch test to make sure you're not allergic to the oil.

Overall, essential oils can be a great natural remedy for aging skin. By using the right oils, you can help reduce the signs of aging and improve the overall health and appearance of your skin.

YOGURT FACE MASKS

Are you looking for a natural and affordable way to nourish your skin? Look no further than your fridge! Full cream yogurt is not only a delicious snack, but it also has amazing benefits for your skin. Using it as a face mask can help to soothe, moisturise, and brighten your complexion.

The lactic acid in yogurt gently exfoliates and removes dead skin cells, revealing fresh, glowing skin. It also contains probiotics that can help to balance the skin's microbiome, promoting a healthy and radiant complexion.

The fat in full cream yogurt provides deep hydration, leaving your skin feeling soft and supple.

In addition, yogurt contains vitamins and minerals such as zinc, vitamin B2, and calcium, which all contribute to healthy skin. It's a natural and gentle alternative to harsh chemicals and synthetic ingredients in many skincare products.

This has been one of my favourite natural face masks and treatments since I was 18. It is perfect for any skin type especially sensitive skin, sunburnt skin or skin that is dry and red from too much heating, air conditioning or has windburn.

HAIR CARE

When it comes to hair care, there are a variety of treatments available that can help improve the health and appearance of your hair. Two of the most common treatments are protein treatments and conditioners. While both treatments can be beneficial for your hair, they work in different ways and are best suited for different types of hair.

Protein Treatments:
Protein treatments are designed to strengthen the hair by adding protein back into the hair shaft. Hair is made up of protein, and daily styling, exposure to heat, and chemical treatments can all cause damage that can weaken the hair. Protein treatments work by penetrating the hair shaft and filling in gaps or breaks in the protein structure, helping to strengthen the hair from the inside out. Protein treatments are best suited for those with weak, damaged, or chemically treated hair.

Conditioners:
Conditioners, on the other hand, are designed to moisturise and detangle the hair. They work by coating the hair shaft with a protective layer that helps to prevent damage and keep the hair hydrated. Conditioners can be used daily to keep the hair soft, smooth, and easy to manage. They are best suited for those with normal to dry hair that is not overly damaged.

While both protein treatments and conditioners can be beneficial for your hair, it's important to choose the right treatment for your hair type and needs. Using a protein treatment on hair that is already strong and healthy can actually cause damage, as too much protein can make the hair brittle and prone to breakage.

Similarly, using a conditioner on hair that is severely damaged may not be enough to restore its health.

If you're not sure which treatment is right for your hair, it's best to consult with a hair care professional who can help you choose the best products and treatments for your specific hair type and needs.

HAIR CARE FOOD - CASTOR OIL

Deep treatment and hair growth Castor oil is my favourite deep conditioning treatment and is a natural oil that has been used for centuries for its numerous health and beauty benefits. One of its most popular uses is for hair care. Castor oil is packed with nutrients, including fatty acids, vitamin E, and minerals, which work together to nourish and strengthen your hair. Here are some of the benefits of using castor oil on your hair and scalp:

1. Promotes hair growth: Castor oil contains ricinoleic acid, which has been shown to stimulate hair growth. Massaging castor oil onto your scalp can help improve blood circulation, which in turn can promote hair growth.

2. Prevents hair loss: The fatty acids in castor oil help to nourish and strengthen hair follicles, which can prevent hair loss.

3. Moisturises dry scalp: Castor oil is a natural moisturiser that can help hydrate a dry, itchy scalp. It can also help soothe any inflammation or irritation caused by scalp conditions like dandruff or eczema.

4. Conditions hair: Castor oil is a great natural conditioner that can help soften and smooth hair. It can also help repair split ends and reduce frizz.

5. Improves hair texture: Using castor oil regularly can help improve the texture and appearance of your hair. It can make hair shinier, thicker, and more manageable.

To use castor oil on your hair and scalp, simply warm up the oil in your hands and massage it into your scalp and hair. Leave it on for at least 30 minutes (or overnight for a more intensive treatment), then rinse it out with shampoo. For best results, use castor oil at least once a week. I also love using castor oil as a deeply penetrating oil for my face several times a week. It's thick, so leave it on to soak in.

ARGAN OIL - for daily use

Argan oil has been used for centuries in Morocco for its numerous health and beauty benefits. When used as a hair moisturiser, argan oil can help to nourish and repair damaged hair, making it softer, shinier, and more manageable. Rich in vitamin E and fatty acids, argan oil helps to hydrate and moisturise the scalp, which can reduce itching and flaking while promoting healthy hair growth.

Unlike many other hair moisturisers, argan oil is non-greasy and quickly absorbed by the hair, leaving it feeling lightweight and silky smooth. Its natural antioxidants help to protect hair from environmental damage, such as pollution and UV rays, which can cause hair to become dry and brittle over time.

To use argan oil as a hair moisturiser, simply apply a few drops to the palms of your hands and massage into your hair, focusing on the ends and any areas that are particularly dry or damaged. It is perfect for daily use and to tame frizzy hair and flyaway ends. With regular use, you'll notice that your hair looks and feels healthier, stronger, and more radiant.

BODY HEALTH -MAGNESIUM BATHS

Magnesium is a mineral that plays a critical role in a wide range of bodily functions, from muscle and nerve function to heart health and bone strength. However, many people don't get enough magnesium through their diets, which can lead to a range of health issues, including muscle cramps, insomnia, and anxiety. One way to boost your magnesium levels is through regular baths, foot soaks, or sprays. Here are some of the benefits:

1. Relieves Muscle Tension: Magnesium helps to relax muscles and relieve tension, making it an effective treatment for sore muscles, cramps, and spasms. A warm bath or foot soak infused with magnesium can be particularly soothing after a workout or long day on your feet.

2. Promotes Relaxation: Magnesium has a calming effect on the nervous system, which can help to promote relaxation and improve sleep quality. Soaking in a magnesium bath before bed can be especially helpful for those who struggle with insomnia or anxiety.

3. Reduces Inflammation: Magnesium has anti-inflammatory properties that can help to reduce pain and inflammation in the body. This makes it a useful treatment for conditions like arthritis and joint pain.

4. Boosts Skin Health: Magnesium is also beneficial for the skin, helping to improve hydration, reduce inflammation, and prevent acne. A magnesium foot soak or spray can be particularly helpful for dry, cracked heels or fungal infections.

5. Increases Absorption: Soaking in a magnesium bath or foot soak can be a more effective way to boost your magnesium levels than taking oral supplements, as it allows the mineral to be absorbed directly through the skin.

BODY HEALTH - MILK BATHS

 Milk baths have been a popular skincare treatment for centuries, and for good reason. Milk is rich in lactic acid, vitamins, and minerals that can help nourish and rejuvenate the skin. Here are some of the skin benefits of taking a milk bath:

1.   Moisturises the skin: The fats and proteins in milk can help hydrate and moisturise the skin, leaving it feeling soft and smooth.

2.   Exfoliates dead skin cells: The lactic acid in milk can help gently exfoliate the skin, removing dead skin cells and revealing brighter, more radiant skin.

3.   Soothes irritated skin: Milk contains anti-inflammatory properties that can help soothe and calm irritated skin, making it a great option for those with eczema, psoriasis, or other skin conditions.

4.   Improves skin tone and texture: The vitamins and minerals in milk, such as vitamin D and calcium, can help improve skin tone and texture, reducing the appearance of fine lines and wrinkles.

5.   Promotes relaxation: Taking a milk bath can be a relaxing and indulgent experience, helping to reduce stress and promote a sense of well-being.

 To take a milk bath, simply add a box of full cream milk powder to warm bathwater and soak for 20-30 minutes. For added benefits, you can also add other natural ingredients like honey, oatmeal, or essential oils. However, if you have any allergies or skin sensitivities, be sure to test any new ingredients on a small patch of skin before using them in a full bath.

SKIN CARE - MY FAVE NATURAL BODY OILS

Macadamia nut oil is a luxurious and deeply nourishing oil that is quickly becoming a popular choice for body skin moisturising. It is packed with essential fatty acids, vitamins, and antioxidants that provide a wealth of benefits for the skin.

One of the main benefits of macadamia nut oil is its ability to deeply moisturise the skin. The oil is easily absorbed and provides long-lasting hydration, helping to keep the skin soft, smooth, and supple. It is also high in oleic acid, a monounsaturated fatty acid that is essential for maintaining healthy skin.

In addition to its moisturising properties, macadamia nut oil is also known for its anti-inflammatory and anti-aging benefits. It contains antioxidants such as vitamin E and squalene, which help to protect the skin from damage caused by free radicals and environmental stressors.

Macadamia nut oil can also help to improve the appearance of scars and stretch marks. Its high concentration of palmitoleic acid can help to boost collagen production and promote healthy skin cell turnover, reducing the appearance of blemishes and promoting a more even skin tone.

One of my favourite ways to use oil on my skin is right after a shower. With my skin still damp, I apply the oil all over my body and the water helps it spread easily. Then I gently pat dry with a towel, allowing the oil to soak in and provide nourishment. It's a luxurious and deeply hydrating experience that leaves my skin feeling soft, smooth, and glowing.

Coconut oil isn't just a kitchen staple, it's also a natural and effective body moisturiser. With its rich, creamy texture, coconut oil can leave your skin feeling soft, supple and nourished.

Coconut oil contains medium-chain fatty acids that penetrate deep into the skin to provide hydration and protection against environmental stressors. It also has anti-inflammatory and antioxidant properties, which can help to soothe and protect your skin from damage.

Using coconut oil as a body moisturiser is a great way to hydrate and nourish dry, flaky or irritated skin. It can also help to reduce the appearance of fine lines and wrinkles, making it a great anti-aging treatment.
In addition to its moisturising benefits, coconut oil can also be used as a natural shaving cream, massage oil and even a hair mask to promote healthy, shiny locks.

Jojoba oil is an excellent natural moisturiser that offers numerous benefits for the skin. Extracted from the seeds of the jojoba plant, this oil is rich in vitamins and minerals that nourish the skin and help combat the effects of aging. Jojoba oil is very similar in composition to the sebum produced by our skin, making it an ideal moisturiser for all skin types.

One of the most significant benefits of using jojoba oil as a body moisturiser is its ability to deeply hydrate the skin without leaving a greasy residue. Its lightweight texture allows it to penetrate the skin quickly, leaving it soft and supple. Jojoba oil is also an excellent emollient, which means it can help soothe dry, itchy, or irritated skin.

Jojoba oil is also rich in antioxidants that help protect the skin from damage caused by free radicals, which can accelerate the aging process. Regular use of jojoba oil can help improve the overall health and appearance of the skin, reducing the appearance of fine lines, wrinkles, and age spots.

Additionally, jojoba oil has anti-inflammatory properties that can help reduce redness and inflammation associated with skin conditions such as eczema, psoriasis, and rosacea. It also contains natural antimicrobial properties that can help fight off bacteria, viruses, and fungi that can cause skin infections.

The Power of Tribing

 Social genomics is a field of study that explores the ways in which social factors can impact gene expression and, ultimately, health outcomes. One area of particular interest within social genomics is the role of tribe or community in shaping our health and well-being.

 Research has shown that our social networks can have a profound effect on our biology, including the expression of genes involved in inflammation, immune function, and stress response. Being part of a supportive and nurturing tribe can have positive effects on our health, while feeling isolated or excluded from a community can have negative impacts.

In fact, studies have suggested that the benefits of a strong tribe or social support network can extend beyond psychological well-being to include physical health outcomes such as reduced risk of chronic diseases and even longer lifespan.

So, if you are interested in optimising your health and well-being, it may be worth considering how you can cultivate a supportive tribe or community around you. This could involve joining social groups or clubs that align with your interests, reaching out to old friends or family members, or volunteering for causes that you care about. By building strong social connections, you may be able to tap into the power of social genomics and boost your overall health and vitality.

As I reflect on the journey I have shared with you in "60 is the new 40," I am filled with gratitude for the women and men who have been there for me through the years. These wonderful humans have taught me the power of tribing, the strength of sisterhood, and the importance of supporting one another.

Growing up with a narcissistic mother who was emotionally and physically abusive, I felt alone and isolated. But as I grew older, I discovered the power of surrounding myself with people who truly saw me, heard me, and supported me.

Through tribing I found a sense of community, belonging, and purpose that has enriched my life in countless ways.
Tribing is not just a social phenomenon; it's a way of life. It's about creating deep connections, women with other women and men with other men and building a support system that can help us navigate life's challenges with grace and resilience. It's about sharing our stories, our wisdom, and our love, and receiving the same in return.

As a wellbeing and empowerment coach, I have had the privilege of helping other women discover the power of tribing in their own lives. I have seen first hand the transformational impact that comes from building supportive relationships with other women who understand and appreciate our unique experiences and perspectives.

As we age, it's more important than ever to have a community of like minded spiritual beings who can lift us up, inspire us, and help us embrace the full potential of our lives.

So I urge you to seek out your tribe, to build strong connections with other individuals that you resonate with and to support and uplift each other as you journey through life.

Together, we can create a world where aging is celebrated, women are valued, and the power of tribing is recognised as one of the greatest forces for good in our society. Thank you for joining me on this journey.

I am honoured to have shared my journey with you in this book, and I hope that it has inspired you to become an ageing disrupter in your own life.

Full disclosure, I am now divorced from my husband after spending 30 years together. I had to make the difficult decision to free us from our toxic relationship that was no longer serving us.

I have joyously written this book, free from the constraints of disempowerment and addiction that felt like the invisible noose I had around my neck, all the things I used as excuses and allowed to hold me back from reaching my full potential.

I used mind mastery to go cold turkey on all my habits, as I know my mind is a very powerful thing and in my life time, I have always achieved anything I set my mind to.

If you have found value in reading "60 is the New 40", and would like to take your journey of disrupting aging further, I offer one-on-one coaching and a 30-day 60 is the new 40 "Disrupt Aging" challenge.

Through personalised coaching, we can work together to create a tailored plan to help you live your life with bravery and passion, and reach your full potential as an aging disruptor.

Alternatively, my course offers a comprehensive program designed to help you make lasting changes in your life and embrace aging with confidence. If you're interested in either of these options, please don't hesitate to reach out to me for more information.

www.info@suzident.com

www.facebook.com/suzident

www.facebook.com/suzidentspeaker

About the Author

As you hold this book in your hands, I invite you to embark on a journey towards defying age and unlocking your full potential. In these pages, you'll discover the ultimate guide to aging gracefully, with insights and strategies that will help you feel confident, beautiful, and empowered at any age.

The author of this book, Suzi Dent, is a true force to be reckoned with. With a wealth of experience as a multi award-winning makeup and hair artist, a dance fitness instructor at age 46, and a wellness and empowerment coach, Suzi has dedicated her life to helping others live their best lives. Her passion and expertise shine through on every page, as she shares her secrets to staying vibrant, healthy, and happy well into your golden years.

But that's not all. Suzi is also an international award-winning inspirational speaker, captivating audiences around the world with her powerful message of hope and positivity. And as if that weren't enough, she's also a beauty queen at 55 and a model at 54, proving that age is truly just a number.

So if you're ready to take control of your life and redefine what it means to age gracefully, this book is for you. With Suzi as your guide, you'll learn how to embrace your inner beauty, cultivate a positive mindset, and make the most of every moment. Let's defy age together, and show the world that 60 is the new 40!

Made in the USA
Columbia, SC
03 May 2023

16062869R00100